The 10 Best Decisions a Woman Can Make

PAM FARREL

HARVEST HOUSE PUBLISHERS

EUGENE, OREGON

Cover by Left Coast Design, Portland, Oregon

Published in association with the literary agency of Alive Communications, Inc., 7680 Goddard Street, Ste #200, Colorado Springs, CO 80920.

THE 10 BEST DECISIONS A WOMAN CAN MAKE
Copyright © 1999 by Pam Farrel
Published by Harvest House Publishers
Eugene, Oregon 97402
www.harvesthousepublishers.com

ISBN 978-0-7369-2838-0

Library of Congress Cataloging-in-Publication Data
Farrel, Pam, 1959-
    [Woman God can use]
    The 10 best decisions a woman can make / Pam Farrel.
        p. cm.
    Originally published: A woman God can use. 1999.
    Includes bibliographical references.
    ISBN 978-0-7369-0228-1 (pbk.)
    1. Christian women—Religious life. I. Title: Ten best decisions a woman can make. II. Title.
BV4527.F48 2004
248.8'43—dc22   2003021791

Printed in the United States of America

10 11 12 13 14 15 16 / DP-MS / 10 9 8 7 6 5 4 3 2 1

Quality friendships create a quality
sounding board for quality decisions.

All my love to those who have
encouraged me this past year:

The *You Can! Ministries* Speaking Team,

The "Seasoned Sisters,"

The women staff members of *Masterful Living,*

and everyone at Harvest House Publishers.

*How can we thank God enough for you
in return for all the joy we have in the
presence of our God because of you?*

1 THESSALONIANS 3:9

Contents

$\mathcal{D}$ecide to $\mathcal{D}$ecide

*You Make Your Choices and
Your Choices Make You*

$\mathcal{A}$lberta Lee Cox was just in the eighth grade when she wrote: "It's not enough to be good if you have the ability to be better. It's not enough to be very good if you have the ability to be great."[1] I believe women were designed for greatness. However, often on our way to greatness we find ourselves in a depressed, despairing, disillusioned, or discouraged place.

I was at a simple gathering of friends. All of us were standing in the kitchen and chatting, as women often do at a party. Our conversation had drifted to the subject of vital areas of need in women's lives. Just then, a friend, a successful businesswoman, grabbed my hand and said, "Pam, I know a book you should write. Women need a book that shows us how to be successful without being so hard on ourselves! I have a friend who listens to self-help tapes—you know, the ones that say: 'You are the master of your own destiny. You can achieve anything. You are all powerful. You... you...you.' The focus is all wrong! She's been feeding herself for months on this junk, as though she is the god of her own universe or something. She thought it would help boost her self-esteem and empower her, but just the opposite has happened. She just keeps hearing how she can make all her own successes, and when she doesn't have the results the tapes promise, she feels as though she is more of a failure than ever before. I think she's going to end up in a padded cell. She's driving herself to the edge of a nervous breakdown!"

That's where we live. Waves of women's empowerment material are cresting, but most of this material neither empowers nor frees us. Instead, we are burdened with the unrealistic expectation that we are supposed to ride every new wave. Many women just give up. Instead of *making* life happen, instead of chasing the dream of their heart, they just *let* life happen. Day after day, the same old same old rut and routine, living their lives out in quiet desperation.

When you live your life accidentally, just meandering along, don't be surprised if your life becomes an accident. Drifting produces depressing results. Neglect relationships, and you'll see people walking away from you; neglect personal growth, and you'll see others pass you up on the ladder to success; neglect your health, and you'll see your energy and vitality diminish. To *not* decide is to decide, but often the results are tragic. Instead, decide that today you will see life through new eyes.

As I have traveled and spoken on women's issues, I have come to some startling conclusions. The first I knew years ago: Women can do some incredible things with a little equipping, encouragement, and inspiration. But I was surprised by the next conclusion. I speak to some of the most together, tenderhearted, loving, and motivated women in the world. These women are responsible and hardworking. Some are wonderful mothers, others are wonderful businesswomen or ministry-minded leaders, and all are great friends and assets to their communities, yet they often feel fragmented, unsure, and discouraged. I think many of us can relate to them. They need to decide to see themselves and their life through new eyes.

Many of us today also struggle with feeling as if we are one big disappointment to everyone. For the most part, we are exhausted as we frantically try to please everyone in our world: our husbands, our children, our parents, our bosses, our clients, our friends, and our coworkers at work and in volunteer work— all while trying to please God too. Sometimes we might even be trying to please ourselves, but we are usually very low on our list of priorities.

I asked women in a survey who they feel they disappoint most often, and the choices included parents, husbands, children, friends, coworkers, bosses, volunteer or church leaders, themselves, and God. The overwhelming majority marked that they thought they disappointed God most often. That answer ran three to one to the second-place answer. How can this be? If God created us, if God desires friendship with us, if He really is all-sufficient and self-existent in and of Himself, then can it really be so easy to disappoint Him? Or could it be that we have a warped view of what God expects from our lives, our relationships, and us? Do you want to be a woman God can use, but you don't want to feel used up in the process?

The average woman today feels as though her life is like a giant jigsaw puzzle. There are lots of important pieces—she is even convinced there is a beautiful picture—but she's looking for the puzzle box lid because she's not sure where to start or what she's really aiming at.

The scary thing is that our lives are jam-packed with activity as we frantically try to balance all of life's demands. We are trying to please those around us, but most of the time we feel as though we are always letting someone down. Are you one of these women? Do you feel that someone is disappointed in you even as you read the words on this page? Do you wonder if God is pleased with your life? Are you pleased with your life? Are you wondering, "Is this all there is to life?" Have you been pushing yourself headlong and are now wondering, "Why?" or "Was it worth it?" Or maybe you have just been drifting, doing the next thing that came along, and now you find yourself far downstream or off course from the place you thought you'd be at this age or stage of life. Decision number one: Decide to *decide* to make things different!

Mirror, Mirror

In the fairy tale *Snow White,* the queen kept checking in with a mirror to determine her standing in the community. *Mirror, Mirror on the wall, who's the fairest of them all?* When I was a little girl, I always despised the queen. She was dark, foreboding, and selfish. But now I think that's what happens to women who look to a false standard to check on their significance. Every woman is looking in a mirror. The question is, what mirror are we using? We might not stand in front of the mirror in our bathroom, asking "Mirror, Mirror…" but we do look around and compare ourselves to others: to women in books, magazines, movies, or television; to friends who are more talented in areas where we feel insecure; and to mentors and public leaders to whom we ascribe the attributes of "the perfect woman." Sometimes we even compare ourselves to us 10 years ago, 20 years ago, or more. Could it be we need a new mirror?

I needed a new mirror because my expectations, others' expectations of me, and God's expectations all seemed to be jumbled up together. I couldn't tell when realistic expectations stopped and unrealistic expectations started. My mirror was so warped that when I sat down to think and plan, my list grew; when others talked with me, my list grew; and even when I read the Bible, my list grew. Sometimes it felt as though God were making my to-do list longer and longer. Because my perspective was so distorted, I thought God's expectations of me were impossible to fulfill. I found myself consistently angry with Him, even though I knew He loved me.

And it's not just me. I often talk with women who seem upset or depressed because life isn't what they thought or dreamed it would be and they are not sure what to do about it. We need to *decide* that things will be different. We make our choices, and our choices make us. What are some choices you need to make? I pray your decisions will lead you to the life God designed for you—a life full of the future and hope God promises (see Jeremiah 29:11).

One of the most freeing experiences in my life was a set of quiet times I had many years ago. I tried to let God be my mirror as I read passages where He describes people. I looked up all the places in the Bible where the words, "You are…" pop up. I found hundreds of passages that proclaim who God says we are. Then I made a list of the ones that seemed to be direct revelations of what He expects of us. The results gave me a new lease on life! A close friend even said to me, "Pam, what's different about you? You seem happier, less stressed…it's almost as though you aren't as frantic as usual. I don't know, but it seemed that you were trying so hard to make everyone happy all the time. Don't get me wrong. Everyone around you is still doing well and feeling great about you—no, maybe we're all feeling better too. It's like whatever God has done in your life has made you freer and that's allowed us to be freer too."

I thought that observation was pretty amazing because she hadn't known what I'd been studying in my quiet times that year. She wasn't saying I had been legalistic, judgmental, or harsh before, because those characteristics have never been ones I thought were productive. What she was saying is that I discovered a gracious calling and a renewed sense of fulfillment, and it had impacted her life too. That is my hope for you. I hope you gain a wonderful fresh view of yourself as you look at God's view of you and gain a heavenly perspective on life. I truly believe women are more successful with their goals and dreams if they have an accurate view of God and a clear reflection of how He sees them.

The by-product from this vital connection with God is that we then can truly find, focus in on, and fulfill His significant calling on our lives because we will know what is significant to Him. We will be women God can use in truly amazing ways.

Can We Really Have It All?

Sometimes we are our own worst enemy. Our expectations regarding ourselves can easily fall to one extreme or another. While some women are on welfare, on drugs, sleeping with men who aren't good for them, ignoring their children, and really aren't caring what anyone expects from them, most women fall in the other extreme—they care too much. Patsy Clairmont, author and Women of Faith conference speaker, says, "We wouldn't care so much what people thought of us if we realized how little they do!" [2] This concern over how other people view us feeds into the fact that we are our own harshest critics. I asked women to tell me their description of a woman who "has it all." These are my favorites because they made me smile:

She is never running late or misplacing anything. Well, I can never be a woman who has it all then because there are days I hunt for car keys, lost cleats, the pancake spatula, and sometimes my kids or husband.

She's unwrinkled. This one knocks all of us over 40 right out of the running.

She has a perfect figure. Okay, this one's tough because it keeps changing! Marilyn Monroe wore a size 16, and I think supermodels today shop in the toddler section. Isn't beauty supposed to be in the eye of the beholder? Maybe that's it—everyone needs to get special 3-D glasses, and maybe then I'd have that elusive "perfect figure."

She is talented, gorgeous, and wealthy with an easy life and no job, and she is the mother of three well-adjusted kids. This one is a classic example of what we do to ourselves all the time—contradict our values. If I were talented and gorgeous with wealth I didn't have to earn, would I really have three *well-adjusted* kids? (And why three kids?) And if I were so wonderfully talented, wouldn't I want to use my gifts in some way? Would I be well-adjusted if I had "an easy life"? I have experienced just the opposite. Women who have gone through hardship and come out on the other side are some of the easiest women to be around because they are low-maintenance women. Their expectations are grounded in the real world.

She's on top of the world. Everything always goes in her favor. She never fails. Never? Some of the women I have met, interviewed, or read about in history have had lives filled with failures and setbacks. Often those very failures became part of the fiber that formed them into a woman God could use in a significant way. Helen Keller was left a blind deaf-mute by a childhood illness. She definitely didn't have it all—she had almost nothing—yet she became one of the most famous women of the twentieth century because she overcame what seemed to be insurmountable obstacles. She gives us this glimpse into her success: "When one door of happiness closes, another opens: but often we look so long at the closed door that we do not see the one which has been opened for us." In my own life, I have found that when I hit obstacles, failures, and roadblocks, it is then that I am in the classroom of heaven and I learn more about who God is and who He says I am.

She's someone who has a maid that someone else *pays for!* (This is my all-time favorite description of a woman who has it all, and I think I hear a hearty *Amen!* rising from women across the world on that one!)

This one was followed closely with: *She's a woman who has plenty of babysitters.* But the one who sums up "the woman who has it all" wrote: *June Cleaver. You know the rest!* Oh yes, the June Cleaver-Carol Brady-Clair Huxtable-Jill Taylor syndrome. Every generation of television watchers has their icons. The problem is some of the people we put on a pedestal are not even real women, and we really want to keep up there the ones who are. The real women, like Martha, Oprah, and Dr. Laura, only give us a glimpse of their everyday lives. We don't walk in their shoes, so we don't really know all the choices, regrets, and feelings they might be experiencing. Oprah Winfrey, who tops the American talk show circuit and sits at the helm of a multimillion-dollar empire, said once, "People think because you're on TV you have the world by a string. But I have struggled with my own self-value for many many years."[3] Oftentimes we simply glamorize these women, and that makes the bar we must hurdle ourselves over even higher.

The "Martha Stewart" Syndrome

Because we all have friends in our lives who seem to have a knack for creating a wonderful atmosphere around them, we sometimes think we must also have that same ability or we've failed. A friend with two small toddlers at home e-mailed me this letter to help us both lighten up a bit on our own expectations:

> A Letter from Martha Stewart!
> Monday, 9:00 A.M.
>
> Hi, Sandy:
>
> This perfectly delightful note is being sent on paper I made myself to tell you what I have been up to. Since it snowed last night, I got up early and made a sled with old barn wood and a glue gun. I hand-painted it in gold leaf, got out my loom, and made a blanket in peaches and mauves. Then, to make the sled complete, I made a white horse to pull it from some DNA I just had sitting around

my craft room. By then, it was time to start making the place mats and napkins for my 20 breakfast guests. I'm serving the old standard Stewart 12-course breakfast, but I'll let you in on a little secret: I didn't have time to make the table and chairs this morning; I used the ones I had on hand. Before I moved the table into the dining room, I decided to add just a touch of the holidays. So I repainted the room in pinks and stenciled gold stars on the ceiling.

Then, while the homemade bread was rising, I took antique candle molds and made the dishes (exactly the same shade of pink) to use for breakfast. These were made from Hungarian clay, which you can get in almost any Hungarian craft store. Well, I must run. I need to finish the buttonholes on the dress I'm wearing for the breakfast. I'll get out the sled and drive this note to the post office as soon as the glue dries on the envelope I'll be making. Hope my breakfast guests don't stay too long—I have 40,000 cranberries to string with bay leaves before my speaking engagement at noon. It's a good thing.

Love,

Martha

P.S. When I made the ribbon for this typewriter, I used 1/8-inch gauze. I soaked it in a mixture of white grapes and blackberries which I grew, picked, and crushed last week just for fun!

I don't know who wrote this original caricature of Martha, but the author understood the "Martha Stewart" syndrome of high expectations we often experience. In all fairness to the real Martha Stewart, she has done a wonderful job of releasing women to be creative (and in recent years she's had her own set of issues to deal with—so reality reminds us it isn't all about having a life that is magazine glossy).

The bigger question is: Why do we, as women, feel bad about ourselves when we see a woman using her God-given gifts and talents well? Why do we sometimes feel that if we are not doing the same thing in the same way, we must be a failure? Why do some of us fall into a pattern of jealousy or, worse, apathy, if our life isn't what we see in others' lives? Decide to decide that you will not fall prey to the negative but rather choose to make some positive changes to gain the life you have always dreamed of, or, better yet, the one God has dreamed up for you!

What Do We Think Is Significant?

To start with, we need to decide some things. Ask yourself: What really is significant to me personally? What is my unique contribution to the lives of others? What are those most significant relationships in my life and how can I protect them?

I surveyed hundreds of women in several states and asked them to respond to some questions. One of the questions was: "What is your definition of significance?" Over half of those responding included the words: "making a difference," "impacting others," or "enacting some kind of a change." Half of the women felt that if something is significant it benefits others. About one in six said that something significant was important or outstanding. About 10 percent tagged on that if significance were truly significant, it had to have eternal value or it had to somehow please God. The words "positive," "special," and "meaningful" were also commonly used in the definitions. About one-quarter of the respondents defined significance in a way that was personal for them. Below are some of their definitions. Which ones do you connect with?

Major, a really big deal
Being different

Having a purpose
100 percent
Significance is relational
Passionate to you
Exceptional, beyond ordinary
When I have finished something I worked very hard doing
  (giving birth was significant!)
An event worth retelling
Uplifting
A wow!

One respondent really took this a step further:

Significance is an influence or a life-changing experience
like:
  Comfort when comfort is needed
  Support when support is needed
  Encouragement when encouragement is needed
  Laughter when laughter is needed
  Tears when tears are needed
  To be there when needed

This beautifully written poem contains a wonderful sentiment, as did most of the definitions I received. Some of you read the words above and knew instinctively how to apply them to life. Many of you, however, may have found the definitions intangible. For example, how would a woman *know* when and what was *needed*? I find that this is one of the most confusing issues in a woman's life. There are so many needs—how can one person fill them? What is average, let alone above average or superior? What exactly constitutes "a wow!" (Sometimes this is easier, because people will actually say *"Wow!"* when they hear of something amazing, special, or meaningful.)

I especially liked these two:

> *I think everything I do as long, as I let God lead me, is significant.*
>
> *Significance must be defined by who we are and not what we do.* (And to that I say "Ditto!" The premise of this book is to help us gain a more heavenly perspective so we can see things from a better and broader point of view and make decisions that will have a positive impact on us and our loved ones.)

We Are More than a Résumé

The problem of seeing ourselves as the sum of our work, however, is epidemic. John Robinson and Geoffrey Godbey, authors of *A Time for Life,* note that "Many Americans have become virtual walking résumés, defining themselves only by what they do."[4] We are more than the sum total of our dossier. Os Guinness calls us all to replace "You are what you do" with "Do what you are."[5] The goal of this book is to help you discover who and what you are, and then you can make decisions based on that calling. This approach leads to wiser choices and a life where we sense God's pleasure—and that is significant.

Are you sensing why our heads are swimming? Why our Day-Timers are jammed with to-do lists? Why we might be feeling that we are very busy and yet wondering if we are accomplishing anything of value? Significance is so subjective. What is significant to one may be insignificant to another.

When I was a competitive gymnast and diver, I was judged by a panel of men and women and then given a score. It was common for the same dive, the same vault, or the same routine to receive a variety of scores. Each judge was receiving the same information, but a large or small mistake was subject to his or her view, his or her liking, his or her priorities. Significance is like that. So often we feel that our lives are being judged by a panel—husband, friends, leaders, church members, coworkers, bosses, children—and all of these people look at us from their own point of view. Because the judging is subjective, each gives us a different score.

The many voices in our lives can sometimes be a distraction that keeps us from truly sensing the significant. When you listen to too many voices, significance starts to become elusive. You don't know whom to please. But God's view of you is concrete. Genuine significance is rooted and grounded in Him.

A significant woman bases her identity on who God says she is, and she is committed to do nothing more and nothing less than what her identity demands. In other words, as I line up my thoughts to God's thoughts about me, I will become a woman He can use. When I see myself through His eyes, I realize my value. I am nothing more than a woman saved by His grace, but I am nothing less than a new creation.

When I see myself through God's eyes, I realize His plan for me is found only in obedience. I am nothing more than a servant and am nothing less than an ambassador. I'm not the master, so I don't make up the rules. There is one God, and it's not me! All that He requires from a servant is obedience—there is nothing more I can add. Being an ambassador opens up opportunities. The more God can trust me, the more He will entrust to me. So anything less than obedience means I risk missing out on precious pieces of His plan for me.

When I see myself through God's eyes, I realize my calling and that He has a unique place for me. If I am driven to do more than my calling, then I'm not being the me God designed. If I am so busy trying to be someone else, then who is being me? If in fear I do less than my calling, I miss out on the adventure of being me. Nothing more and nothing less will gain God's applause for me. Decide to make the decision: *God, I will be whom You created me to be. Nothing more, nothing less, than being the best possible unique me! I am deciding to line my life up with Your view of me. I choose a connection with You so I can connect to what You have for me.*

Today, decide that *you will decide.* Don't let life happen—*make* life happen! Decisions move you forward by a series of wise choices. Decide to choose. Victorian novelist George Eliot was ahead of her time when she wrote, "It is never too late to be what you might have been." Decide to be different. Decide to make things different.

Plug In Instead of Plugging Along

As I nurture my connection to God, I gain the desire, ability, and motivation to obey. Out of obedience I will sense and experience a life of significance. When I agree with God's view of me, I gain the ability to grasp which opportunities are significant from heaven's vantage point. I see which relational connections are significant from His box seat on high. I even see what daily, seemingly insignificant actions and decisions might have significant impact from an eternal perspective. As I see myself from God's point of view, the pieces fall together easier because God holds the box top to the puzzle. He already sees the completed picture of me and my life. My relationship with Him is the key that unlocks the puzzle's solution. Each decision will put a piece in place. Decide you will decide to put the pieces of your life together. Now, let's sort out the pieces—and find the framework for your life.

Decision Points

How would you describe a woman who "has it all"? How is the description different from your life right now?

Reflect on this thought: We make our choices and our choices make us. What are some wise choices you have made? What are some choices you should have made as you look back? What choices do you want to make to move forward?

You Are...

Sometimes we forget to look at ourselves through God's eyes. Place this list somewhere you can see it often. You are...

The salt of the earth	
The light of the world	Matthew 5:13-14
More valuable than birds	Luke 12:24
In Me and I in you	John 14:20; 17:21
Already clean	John 15:3
The branches	John 15:5
My friends	John 15:14
Heirs of the prophets and of the covenant	Acts 3:25
Servants of the Most High	Acts 16:17
Called	Romans 1:6-7
Weak in your natural selves	Romans 6:19
Still worldly	1 Corinthians 3:2-4
God's fellow workers, God's field, and God's building	1 Corinthians 3:9
God's temple	1 Corinthians 3:16-17
Strong, honored	1 Corinthians 4:10
A temple of the Holy Spirit	1 Corinthians 6:19
Standing firm	1 Corinthians 10:12-13
Part of the body of Christ	1 Corinthians 12:27
A letter from Christ	2 Corinthians 3:1-3
Christ's ambassador	2 Corinthians 5:20
Sons of God	Galatians 3:26
Abraham's seed	Galatians 3:28-29
Sons, an heir	Galatians 4:6-10
Children of the promise	Galatians 4:27-28
Fellow citizens and members of God's household	Ephesians 2:19
Children of the light	Ephesians 5:8
Standing firm	1 Thessalonians 3:8
Sons of the light and sons of the day	1 Thessalonians 5:4-5
Slow to learn	Hebrews 5:11
Mist	James 4:14
Living stones	1 Peter 2:5
A chosen people, a royal priesthood, and a holy nation	1 Peter 2:9-10
Daughters of Sarah	1 Peter 3:6

2

Decide to Be Authentic

Discovering and Living Out
Your God-Given Potential

Television talk show host Chris Chubbuck scripted her own death and carried it out by putting a gun to her head and pulling the trigger as horrified viewers watched. The 29-year-old anchorwoman died in a hospital 14 hours later in Sarasota, Florida.

Her handwritten, blood-spattered script read, "Today Chris Chubbuck shot herself during a live broadcast." Following the incident, the Sarasota sheriff's office and station WXLT were swamped with calls from viewers who could not believe the shooting had been real. It was real. A real woman, who seemed to be on top of the world, felt that she wasn't. Women everywhere on a daily basis make similar life-altering, self-destructive choices because the pieces of their lives seem to be falling apart. Maybe you have never put a gun to your head, but have you shortchanged yourself because you were afraid, unsure, or insecure? Have you ever told yourself that happily-ever-afters are for other women, not you? Have you accepted the status quo rather than reaching up? Have you thought your dreams would come true if you were only smarter, taller, thinner, or richer?

How Discontentment Began

Discontentment started with one woman knowing the plan but not believing it was the real key to happiness. One woman listening to lies and believing them to be truth. One woman rejecting

God's view of significance and embracing a false promise. It sounded good, but it was bad—real bad. That woman was Eve.

One day after Eve had walked with God and enjoyed the perfect garden He had created for her and Adam, she stopped by to chat with a crafty serpent. He must have been charming, intriguing, and engaging. He said to Eve, "Did God really say, 'You must not eat from any tree in the garden'?" Strike one.

Then Eve repeated the instructions she knew so well. "I am not to eat the fruit of this tree or I will die." So the serpent pulled out his most convincing lie. "You will not surely die," he said to the woman. "For God knows that when you eat of it your eyes will be opened, and you will be like God, knowing good and evil." Strike two.

Then Eve acted on this wrong information. She knew it was the opposite of what God said. She was fully aware of her choice but unaware of its consequences. "When the woman saw that the fruit of the tree was good for food and pleasing to the eye, and also desirable for gaining wisdom, she took some and ate it. She also gave some to her husband, who was with her, and he ate it." Strike three—we're out!

It wasn't long before the reality of it all hit. "Then the eyes of both of them were opened, and they realized they were naked; so they sewed fig leaves together and made coverings for themselves. Then the man and his wife heard the sound of the Lord God as he was walking in the garden in the cool of the day, and they hid from the Lord God among the trees of the garden.

"But the Lord God called to the man, 'Where are you?'" Later God said to Eve, "'What is this you have done?'"

Eve said, "The serpent deceived me, and I ate." And the consequences of her embrace of false significance have laid the foundation for all of us to be prone to the same deceptions. (See Genesis 3:1-13.)

We can't entirely blame her. We are all prone to watching out for our own interests—and that's what got Eve into trouble in the first place. First John 2:15-16 lays out three similar ways we fall for false significance:

"Do not love the world or anything in the world. If anyone loves the world, the love of the Father is not in him. For everything in the world—[1] the cravings of sinful man, [2] the lust of his eyes and [3] the boasting of what he has and does—comes not from the Father but from the world." Our flesh wants to be fulfilled, and then our eyes want what we see, and then we want something to brag about. Eve fell for the same three things. *It feels so good:* Her flesh wanted the fruit. *It looks so good:* Her eyes saw the new plan Satan laid out—and she wanted it. *It sounds so good:* Then she fell for the big one. "You can be like God." Now that would be something to brag about—but it was all lies. And we can fall for the same lies today. Life still turns inside out when false principles of significance are embraced.

Do You Really Want a Storybook Life?

There are so many false places of significance we can be lured and lulled into, thinking we are attaining some real significance. After all, women are almost trained to look in the wrong places. For example, let's examine some of the common storybook characters many of us grew up on. There is sweet, naïve Sleeping Beauty, who has to wait for a prince to come along and kiss her in order for her to wake up and be free to live. Little Red Riding Hood, poor thing, just couldn't follow directions about not going through the forest and is eaten by a wolf, and a woodchopper has to kill the wolf and free Red Riding Hood and Granny. Rapunzel at least took her destiny in her own hands and decided she wasn't going to be locked in a tower anymore, but she had to use her gorgeous good looks (her hair) as the means to gain a new life.

And then there's Goldilocks. She is a picture of many women today, flitting from thing to thing to thing, looking for something that will make her life "just right." Like Goldilocks, we are looking for significance in all the wrong places.

To be authentic women who can *decide* to reach our God-given potential, we have to be willing to take a long look in the mirror and ask: Which false sense of significance am I vulnerable to believing?

Because my husband, Bill, and I also write marriage books, I work with many women who search for significance in a man. Sometimes these women come into my office because they grow tired of being beaten, sometimes they fear for the lives of their children, sometimes they are tossed aside for a younger woman or left by an already irresponsible husband as he steps out of their life in search of the next party. What amazes me is that all the women that come to see me have the same opportunity to change their life, to start over again. I explain the processes we must walk women through in order to rebuild their lives, but only about half decide to go the distance and allow God to remake their sense of significance. The others simply meet another guy, usually while they are out dancing or at a bar, and they sleep with him and start the same bad cycle all over again.

Without some structured help, the cycle won't stop. Only a direct intervention from heaven will reach down and break the destructive pattern. Only unconditional love from the Father will take your battered heart, bandage it up, and give you a new identity. It can be hard work to allow God to rebuild your sense of significance, but it is harder work to not allow Him to rebuild your life!

If you are single, complete the chart on page 27 as a safeguard to keeping your significance coming from your relationship with God rather than from any man. Make a list in the first column of traits you'd like in a future spouse (this is how God would treat

How Can I Decide?		
Attributes	*Green Light*	*Red Light*
Character traits I want in the person I marry someday.	How can I tell the trait is there?	How can I tell the trait is NOT there?

you!), and then write down how you will know the man has the trait, and finally write down clues so you'll know if he does *not* have the trait. This will serve as a grid so you can logically think through any future relationships. For example: In the attributes column I might have: *Respects women.* In the green-light column: *He listens to me when I talk, he respects my personal boundaries and physical standards, and he is a gentleman with polite behavior.* In the red-light column (which means address these if they come up and run the other way if there is little change or too many red lights): *It might be the way he talks about his mother. He doesn't keep his promises.*

Power

Power is so subtle as it weaves a web around your heart. Power can begin with such good intentions. A job promotion, a new career opportunity, a new business adventure, the thrill of owning your own company are all very good things that can also become deceptive traps of false significance. Becoming accustomed to external rewards may cause internal rewards to pale in significance. The nameplate, the business award, the company perks may become more important than God's still, small voice wooing you to Himself.

Most women never set out to put a career ahead of a husband, a child, a ministry, or a relationship with God. It happens so gradually that it would be like watching grass grow or water in a kettle boil. The change can be hard to discern—but usually you sense the change. Things you previously wouldn't have accepted you now rationalize as okay, necessary, or even good.

Several years ago, a woman, Gina, came to me. She was worried about her three daughters. One was out of the house, living with a boyfriend, the next two were 15 and 13, and she was concerned about their grades, choices of friends, and so on. I asked her about their lives and then her own. I found out that she was gone from the house from 6 A.M. until 7 or 8 P.M. every day, as was her husband. Her two youngest daughters were unsupervised from 2:15 until 7 or 8 P.M. I mentioned that she or her husband might consider a career shift, and I suggested tag-team parenting, job sharing, and part-time work as possible solutions so the girls could have more direct time with their parents. I could tell that Gina was struggling with these suggestions.

To make a long story painfully short: Over the years I have seen the oldest two daughters become pregnant at young ages and outside of marriage. The third ended up in juvenile hall for a time. Gina continued to work, and eventually she also had an affair and abandoned her husband and daughters for the other man. I recently saw her. She is in an unhappy marriage, in a job that still eats up all of her time, and she looks twice her age. Yes, Gina climbed a couple of rungs up the career ladder, but she did so at too high a price. She gained some external significance in a temporal way, but she has never found significance that lasts, the kind that brings hope, peace, and joy.

When I began writing from home, I asked God to show me a red flag in each one of my boys that I could pick up on so I would be able to visibly see if they were carrying stress that wasn't theirs. After I prayed I noticed the red flag with Brock when he became more distant emotionally. Zach's red flag was easy to spot; he would become grumpy and sloppy. Caleb grew tired and whiney.

How about you? Is your working interfering with some of the other things you value in life? If so, how? Brainstorm a list of ways to keep your career in check. How will you know if it is becoming too important to you? Ask God to search your heart to see if too much of your identity and significance are being derived from your career. When we are working in our God-given talent area— our uniqueness—we are fulfilled, but when our significance is derived from the kudos, the compliments, and the connections to power work brings, we are at the edge of the slippery slope to destruction. *Decide* how you will keep a "heart check" in your life so that work remains fulfilling but not all-consuming.

Title

What if all your titles were suddenly taken away from you? Most of us think titles aren't that important to us, yet we'd have a difficult time describing ourselves without them. This is a good heart check for making sure you are doing things for the right reasons. I have been married more than 24 years, and 22 of those I have been a pastor's wife. Then my husband had a health issue, and we had to make some tough career choices. We decided our uniqueness is in the areas of writing and speaking, primarily on relationships, so Bill resigned as pastor. A major title of respect was taken out of my life that day. And it was a double whammy because, in the year before that, I had resigned my job as director of women, a position I held for 13 years. I found myself asking a very important question almost daily: "Pam, are you going to keep doing the things God called you to, even though that title is gone?" It was a great heart check. Authenticity is doing what is right regardless of the circumstances.

It's Not About Prestige

> I commend to you our sister Phoebe, a servant of the church in Cenchrea. I ask you to receive her in the Lord in a way worthy of the saints and to give her any help she may need from you, for she has been a great help to many people, including me (Romans 16:1-2).

Phoebe is called a sister, a servant. She didn't have business cards or a gold nameplate on her door. She didn't have riches. There is no mention of her owning a Fortune 500 company. She didn't have a title, material possessions, a house at the beach, or a country club card. No, she had something better—Paul's personal recommendation. Phoebe had a good name. Proverbs tells us, "A good name is more desirable than great riches; to be esteemed is better than silver or gold" (Proverbs 22:1). A good name is even better than a write up in *Business Weekly* or the society page. What Phoebe earned was influence.

Money

Making money isn't a bad thing. The problem begins when money grabs your heart and yanks you away from God. One Sunday morning I had a hard time enjoying the music of our worship service, concentrating on the sermon, or praying. I tried to focus on Jesus, but my mind kept hopping back to a business venture I had just committed to. It wasn't a passing preoccupation. I was submerged in deep contemplation about how to make a buck! And I hated it. I decided if I was going to be ripped away from Jesus because of the new business opportunity, it wasn't an opportunity at all but an obstacle. I walked away from that way of money making because the price was too high.

If you lost all your money, how would you feel about yourself? How much money would it take for you to feel secure or complete? Does having money change the way you treat people? Does having money make you feel superior? Is making money or thinking about finances keeping you from other vital priorities (marriage, children, friendships)? Having money is a tool. It should be nothing more.

Looks

A psychological study in 1995 found that three minutes spent looking at models in a fashion magazine caused 70 percent of women to feel depressed, guilty, and shameful. There are three billion women who don't look like supermodels and only about eight who do.

The average American woman weighs 142 lbs., is 5'4", and wears between a size 12 and 14.[1] Models who 20 years ago weighed 8 percent less than the average woman today weigh 23 percent less. The average model is 5'9" and weighs in at 110 lbs.[2] It is no wonder that the average woman feels inadequate, and that one out of every four college-aged women has an eating disorder.

When we take good care of ourselves, that is honoring to God and healthy. But when we obsess about our features, our size, and our fashion IQ, we move from healthy to leaning on our looks for significance.

Do you think you would be a better person if you wore a smaller size? Would your worth go up if you had more money for fashionable clothes? Does the thought of going out without makeup send chills up your spine? Yes, it is very, very important to your long-term health to try to stay close to your medically recommended weight, but are you really trying to be healthy or are you trying to gain fulfillment because you desire heads to turn when you walk into a room? Is your focus on the external short-changing your internal growth?

This false source of significance sneaks up on our hearts. We all want to look and feel our best. We want that first impression to count. But if we're not careful, our priorities about the way we look can slide right into that number one spot. Dieting is a multi-million-dollar industry. I finally found a diet that has rules I can keep. Rules for this diet are:

1. If you eat something and no one sees you eat it, it has no calories.

2. If you drink a diet soda with a candy bar, the calories in the candy bar are canceled out by the diet soda.

3. When you eat with someone else, calories don't count if you do not eat more than they do.

4. Foods used for medicinal purposes *never* count, such as hot chocolate, toast, and Sara Lee Cheesecake.

5. If you fatten up everyone else around you, then you look thinner.

6. Movie-related foods do not have additional calories because they are part of the entertainment package and not part of one's personal fuel. Examples: Milk Duds, Junior Mints, Red Hots, Tootsie Rolls, and buttered popcorn.

7. Cookie pieces contain no calories. The process of breaking causes calorie leakage.

8. Things licked off knives and spoons have no calories if you are in the process of preparing something.

9. Foods that have the same color have the same number of calories. Examples are: spinach and pistachio ice cream, mushrooms and mashed potatoes. Note: Chocolate is a universal color and may be substituted for any other food color.

10. Anything consumed while standing has no calories. This is due to gravity and the density of the caloric mass.

11. Anything consumed from someone else's plate has no calories since the calories rightfully belong to the other person and will cling to his or her plate. (We *all* know how calories like to cling!)

Okay, I'm just kidding! But you laughed because we've all been there. We feel the pressure if we don't measure up to the airbrushed pictures in the magazines—and humor is a way to combat the pain.

I have a question I've asked myself each day since I was in high school, "Pam, are you spending as much time in the Bible as you are in front of the mirror?" God highlights this priority in 1 Peter 3:3-4: "Your beauty should not come from outward adornment, such as braided hair and the wearing of gold jewelry and fine clothes. Instead, it should be that of your inner self, the unfading beauty of a gentle and quiet spirit, which is of great worth in God's sight."

In each chapter, we'll look in God's Word and let Him tell us who we are. Some powerful verses come right after Peter's encouraging words about cultivating inner beauty: "For this is the way the holy women of the past who put their hope in God used to make themselves beautiful. They were submissive to their own husbands, like Sarah, who obeyed Abraham and called him her master. You are her daughters if you do what is right and do not give way to fear" (1 Peter 3:5-6).

"You are her daughters." The emphasis is on what caused the change rather than the change itself. Literally, the original means "you became her daughters." The way we become daughters of Sarah is through a commitment, a *decision,* to developing the habit of doing what is right and not giving in to fear. When we obey God and focus on the internals over the externals of life, we gain a less complicated life. We become low-maintenance women.

Do you know the difference between low-maintenance women and high-maintenance women? Here are a few principles I have taught my boys so they can steer clear of high-maintenance women.

The less clothes a girl has on is directly proportional to the amount of baggage she is carrying emotionally. Little clothes means many bags. She's a high-maintenance woman. A high-maintenance woman puts people in no-win situations. For example, she'll ask, "Do I look fat in this outfit?" If you say yes, she'll burst out in tears. If you say no, she says, "Oh, you have to say that—

you're married to me" or "You're only saying that because I'm your friend."

I'm also giving my boys some pointers on spotting low-maintenance women because I know marriage to a low-maintenance woman is a lot less complicated and less stressful. I call them LM women:

- An LM woman doesn't ask for compliments, but she graciously receives them when given.

- An LM woman knows that *winning* and *whining* are spelled differently and should never be used interchangeably.

- An LM woman doesn't try to wear you down. Instead, she seeks to build you up.

- An LM woman follows as well as she leads.

- An LM woman is more interested in the *team* working than the *theme* working.

- An LM woman knows how to use makeup, but she doesn't hide behind it.

- An LM woman believes personal happiness is a benefit, not a goal or a right.

- An LM woman accepts a man's input without needing his attention.

- An LM woman appreciates her girlfriend's input but doesn't need her approval.

- An LM woman realizes that a bad hair day, a broken nail, a run in the panty hose, or a change in plans are a natural part of the ebb and flow of life, not the makings of a tragic epic suitable for a TV miniseries.

Home and Family

Probably the areas that are easiest to rationalize as true sources of significance are your children and your home. Society honors and values us when our kids turn out well. In Christian circles, motherhood is valued, as it should be, but some women value their children and their role as a mother *too* much. Several pastors' wives and directors of women's ministries have shared with me a dilemma they are experiencing: Mothers are not wanting to attend Bible studies, Sunday school classes, or other women's events because they say their children have to come first. The problem is that the reasoning sounds so biblical, so legitimate. But tragic results occur in the teen years when mom, having not invested in her relationship with God or in interests or ministry outside her family, lacks the emotional, spiritual, and sometimes intellectual strength and information to guide her teens through difficult transitional years.

Sometimes her marriage is even put at risk by this pattern because dad has been out there growing and developing as a person, but mom has been wrapped up with the children.

If we think we cannot live without our children, consider Hannah. She longed for a child, waited for a child, prayed and begged God for a child. Hannah vowed to give the child back to God if He would miraculously place a baby in her barren womb. God took her up on the offer. Hannah conceived and bore a son, Samuel, who, when he was just the age of a preschooler, was given back to God. Samuel grew up under Eli's care and became one of Israel's most celebrated faithful priests.

I think it is the very act of giving our children back to God that allows us to be a tool that God can use to grow them. When we hang on too tightly, our children can become possessions of our hearts rather than precious creations in God's hands.

Ask yourself: "Do I use my children as a shield, a way to get out of personal growth activities like Bible studies, ministries, or volunteer work that would help me discover God or discover the gifts and abilities He's entrusted to me? Am I hiding behind my kids because I have areas I feel insecure in, like interpersonal relationships or leadership?"

Has your home become a showplace rather than a source of ministry? Our homes should be places of order, neat enough to live an organized life, but they should also be places in which anyone would be welcome. How welcome does a toddler feel in your home—or a teen?

It's true for all of us. Significance can't be found in the externals of life—not career, the perfect home, or those wonderful children. Significance can be found only in a person, Christ.

We don't have to hype ourselves up by depending on a title, material possessions, power, or position. You don't have to grapple or claw to hold on to a symbol of prestige. This is a book about attitudes—most importantly, God's attitude toward you. As you come to believe His opinions about you, they will change your attitudes about yourself. Your foundation is secure. You don't have to go searching for significance—you already have a part in His plan!

Finding the Missing Pieces

Sometimes God brings someone into your life to give you a glimpse of how your serving Him is significant from His point of view. The more I encourage women to allow God to rework the way they see themselves, the more excited I am about the results. As their own perspective aligns with God's, hope springs—and out of hope, new life. It's as if they find missing pieces to the puzzle of their life.

I asked Lisa, one of the women God brought into my sphere of influence, to share in her own words the changes that occurred in her heart as she allowed God to reshape her view of herself from heaven's point of view. When I first met Lisa, she looked like a model who had just stepped off the pages of a fashion magazine. Her husband was driving an expensive car, her little boy was dressed like a little GQ man. I wondered why her friend JoAnna had said to me in a private whisper as she hugged me, "Meet my friend Lisa. She is really hurting and needs some help." As I spent time with Lisa, I thought of the quote of Mary Kay Ash, "So many women just don't know how great they are. They come to us all vogue outside and vague on the inside." I was privileged to be a part of watching Lisa take hold of the picture God had of her. These are the words from her heart:

> Once upon a time, there was a little girl who used to lay awake in bed at night listening to the sound of her mother and father yelling, arguing, and sometimes hitting one another. The little girl would say to herself, *Someday my prince is going to come. He is going to carry me away to a faraway castle, and we will live happily ever after.*
>
> That little girl was me. I grew up in a very dysfunctional family. I wanted a fairy-tale life, and I thought a prince was the only way to my dream. A prince would come along, rescue me, and we would have a wonderful life together. Well, my prince came, or at least I thought he was a prince at first, but he turned into a frog. I thought I was a princess who had everything she needed in her prince. Imagine my surprise and disappointment when my fairy tale was ripped away.
>
> You see, my prince was not a prince. I was in denial. I was living a lie in an unhealthy relationship, striving for perfection, only to receive more abuse from a person who was not connected to God. All my life I have struggled with feelings of not being pretty enough, good enough, or smart enough. I strove to feel wanted,

loved, and accepted, and in doing so I set myself up for failure in my relationship with my husband. I truly wanted our relationship to work because, first and foremost, I had made a commitment to God. However, my husband was not willing to participate. Instead of getting help, he chose to abandon the relationship and sought physical comfort elsewhere.

My fairy-tale life crashed down in tiny pieces around my feet, looking like Cinderella's slipper would have if it had been tossed aside onto the hard pavement. I asked myself, *How did this happen? How could I have mistaken a frog for a prince so easily?* My father was an alcoholic, a drug user, and a physical and verbal abuser. I chose my father all over again when I chose my husband. If that's all you know, that's what you attract. But God is so gracious. As I look back, I see how He carried me through some very hard times when I didn't know much about Him.

I remember the feeling of loneliness when my birth mother left and gave me to my father along with my sister and brother to be raised by him. Then I remember my father marrying my step-mother when I was seven. She was my first role model. She was also the first positive influence in my life and I felt, and still do feel, very loved by her. When I was 12, my stepmom could not handle my father's drugs, alcohol, and not coming home at nights, so she chose to leave the relationship for her own safety. There I was again, all alone. The one person whom I trusted in, loved, and connected with had abandoned me. My sister, with whom I was and still am very close, was in and out of my life as a result of my birth mother wanting her whenever she felt lonely. As I went through the experience of my father's second divorce, I was an emotional wreck. I felt everyone in the world had or would abandon me. I was having a nervous breakdown, and I didn't even know it. I went a year and a half stuffing my feelings, not sharing because I was embarrassed, ashamed, and unable to trust anyone.

As I moved forward into my sophomore year in high school, I took a creative writing class as part of the graduation curriculum. It was that class that started my recovery process over the divorce of my parents. I had to write a story about something that had happened to me. I chose to write about my parents' divorce and how it had affected me. I will always admire and respect my teacher for encouraging me the way she did. For the first time in my life, I felt I had a gift—and that gift was writing. I remember saying to myself after I had written my story, *I'm never going to get a divorce when I marry because I never want my children to experience the pain that I have endured.* Just a short time later, my father was put in prison for smuggling cocaine. My sister was sent to live with my birth mother and my brother was placed in a foster home. I moved out of our house and continued my education. I worked to support myself financially. But there I was again, alone!

There was never a safe environment where I could truly run to and call home. I struggled for years. At age 18 my father died of a drug overdose. I felt all alone again, and even felt responsible for his death. I remember thinking, *If only I could have helped him and got him the proper help he needed.* The truth was that I could do nothing—I was just a young girl. He had made the choice on his own to live out his life in that manner, but I carried this burden in my heart for many years.

At age 24 I married my ex-husband. Little did I realize that I would have to relive my father all over again. As I look back, God was faithful to me even as I saw my marriage dissolve. God took me out of a verbally and physically abusive relationship and put me in a loving, safe environment by connecting me with friendships that are more precious than silver. After the police had been summoned to my home in a domestic violence call, my friend Debbie came to get me and I stayed with her. I tried to make my marriage work again, but when I no longer felt safe and was afraid for myself and my little boy, Taylor, she came again and helped me move out of my home to a safe place. I will always appreciate the sacrifices she made for me. God had placed Joanna as my neighbor at that time, and she introduced me to Valley Bible Church, which led to meeting Pam and Bill Farrel. Pam and Joanna introduced me to Penny, who would also become a part of my support team. This team counseled me and helped build and restore my personal relationship with God.

During the course of my recovery, I said, *Okay, God, if You're really there, I want You to develop me, give me confidence, restore my damaged emotions, and show me what Your will is.* One of the first steps of recovery is gathering together a support team of women who all have a strong connection to God. Pam, Penny, and Joanna held me accountable, prayed for me, encouraged me, and cheered me on through the whole process.

As I began my recovery, I could feel God's blessings pouring upon me. I developed an undeniable love that I've never known. God just kept answering every request. I was His precious child. I learned we have a gracious and loving God, who is so willing to give us the desires of our heart if we are willing to abide in Him and be obedient to Him. I began a personal relationship with God, going to Him in prayer many times throughout the day.

Many emotions flooded my thoughts when I was going through the recovery process, but I didn't react emotionally. I had made a choice, a decision, and a commitment to get help. I did not want to repeat the same relationship over again. I didn't want to subject Taylor to any more pain in his life. I took my son to counseling, and I encouraged him to express himself and nurtured his connection to God. I also made sure I was available and present in his life, even when it meant putting my own emotions in God's hands while I cared for his needs. As I raised my son, God allowed me to reflect back on how my own earthly father must have felt as a child. He probably felt the same feelings I went through: loneliness, sadness, anger, and isolation. I never knew my grandfather, but from what I've been told he was an abuser too. It's a vicious cycle. Our behaviors get passed down generation after generation. But God gives each of us the option of choosing Him and breaking the cycle.

One of my first assignments from Pastor Bill was to write about my life. I had lost my desire to write when my ex-husband took my journals without my consent and read them and interpreted them into what he wanted them to read. I have to admit I was somewhat nervous and excited when I was asked to write my story. I remember sitting on my sofa and before I knew it four hours had passed. I felt so alive, so rejuvenated. My passion was back. The gift God had given me was alive, and I felt thankful to be experiencing that desire again.

As a part of the support-group homework, Pam had me choose verses about God and about how He saw me. I began to experience hope again. With the hope grew a desire for a life change. The group had me write down my goals, dreams, and desires. I started charting my journey, asking God to lead me all the way. I hung my goals and desires on my refrigerator and bathroom mirror, as well as placing them in my Day-Timer. Here were some of my personal goals:

1. Restore my damaged emotions

2. Read Bible daily/prayer

3. Job/more income

4. Money to pay taxes

5. Take vacation with Taylor

6. Start saving for new home

7. Spend more time with Taylor—reading, music, fun things

8. New car

God has provided each and every one. Every single goal has been met. One of the verses that I used to have hanging in my apartment was one that I cling to to this day. Mark 11:24: "Therefore, I tell you, whatever you ask for in prayer, believe that you have received it, and it will be yours."

God used my circumstances to show me other women who were in far worse situations than I had been. I remember talking to a woman who was literally in hiding, in fear of her life with two babies. My heart went out to her. I remember saying, *Oh God, how can I help?* At that moment, God put the desire in my heart to start a ministry for single moms. When I consulted with Pam, I found out she had been praying for years for a woman who wanted to reach out to single mothers. I began to see myself as a woman God could use. God was pulling the pieces of my life together. I then stepped out and allowed Him to use me, my heart, and what He had done in my life to encourage other women.

As God continued to rework the way I thought about myself, Him, and life in general, I felt courageous, strong, and positive. I wasn't just dreaming about being a princess—God was showing me I was a daughter of the King of kings. One day I wrote in my journal: God, You know my heart, You know my desires. In Your timing, when You feel I am ready for a relationship, one of my requests is that I not be subjected to unhealthy men. Another request is that when You choose to put a good, solid Christian man in my life, here is a list of qualities and characteristics that I would like to be in that relationship:

1. A man who loves You first before me or anything.

2. Someone who loves Taylor as if he were his own.

3. An excellent communicator.

4. Someone with a sense of humor.

5. Someone sensitive, loving, and caring.

6. A support person who will encourage me in my desires to write and to minister.

7. Someone who will be a good provider.

8. Gee, God, it would be nice if he sang or played an instrument of some sort.

The evening of the day I penned those words in my journal, I was invited to a customer's husband's fiftieth birthday party. I almost didn't make it there because I couldn't find the place, but I eventually arrived about an hour late. I almost turned around, but a voice inside me kept saying, *Go—you never get out, Lisa. Besides, what is so unsafe about a fiftieth birthday party? This is where I want you to be.* Little did I know that this would be the night that I would run into my future husband. I had known John for three years, but we had a business relationship. We both had a rule that we didn't date customers or vendors. Well, John had left the company he was with and was moving to Arizona to accept another position with a different company. At the end of the evening, he asked me out. I said, "Sure, give me a call and we'll set something up."

This was perfect in my mind because he was geographically undesirable. In addition, he wasn't my type. You know, the "prince-type" I had always gone for before: an arrogant, suave, tall, blond-hair, blue-eyed, perfect-body type of guy. Then I remembered, *Lisa, you have been attracted to prince-types before—but they turned out to be frogs. Give this guy a chance. He might have character and be a son of the real Prince of Peace!*

Then I remembered the verse I had posted everywhere during my recovery: "It is better to take refuge in the LORD than to trust in man. It is better to take refuge in the LORD than to trust in princes" (Psalms 118:8-9).

I would have missed John if God hadn't remade my thinking in the months before. No, John wasn't the fairy-tale kind of guy I'd gone for before, but he did meet all the things in my letter to God—so much so that he sang in a choir growing up as a child and he plays the clarinet to this day!

One day during this time, a girlfriend and I were talking and she asked me, "If you were to ever get married again, how would you do it?"

Well, being the dreamer that I am I said to her, "I love yellow. I want to get married in Hawaii, the girls wearing yellow chiffon dresses, barefoot, with French manicures and haku leis around their ankles." I simply set the dream aside, concentrating on more important issues now before me. I didn't want to repeat a dysfunctional relationship, so before John and I became serious, we really took the time to get to know one another. I wanted to make sure this person was a good, solid Christian man, so one of the first things I did was introduce him to my support team. I wanted any man in my life to pass the test of my friends and their husbands. A safety net under my life was when God showed me the value of surrounding myself with a circle of friends—including those solid in their marriages. Everyone in my world loved John, including my son, so we began some extensive premarital counseling before making a commitment. We also decided that our dating life would be run by God's standards, and we committed to not having a sexual relationship prior to our wedding night.

Life is better than a fairy tale. That June, John and I stood in a little green church called Waioli Hui'ia Church in Hanalei, Kauai. Pam and Bill and many of my support team were there as John and I became husband and wife. The ladies wore beautiful yellow chiffon dresses and were barefoot with haku leis around their ankles and necks. The ceremony was a celebration to God and filled with music, the personal vows we wrote for one another, and the commitment of love for a lifetime.

The morning after our wedding, we sat in silence, holding each other. In the distance we could see the ocean waves crashing slowly against the sandy coastline. Piercing through the clouds were beams of light from the sun, and off in the distance was a beautiful rainbow with the most majestic, vibrant colors I had ever seen. We felt the rainbow was God's way of reminding us that He is always faithful to bless those who are faithful to Him. And the rainbows of God's love continue in our marriage and in our growing family. I often reflect back on what started it all, a whisper of God's love telling me, "Lisa, I know you're struggling right now, but trust in Me." I did then, and I do now because He sees me as I was designed to be, and He is daily working out plans to give me a future and a hope.

As you get to know God, He will help you know yourself and know His significant plan for your unique life. When our significance is developed in our relationship with Him, we are free to be good moms, good wives, good career people—and our ability to be good in those areas will come because we don't *need* them for our identity. Because we don't *need* them, we can be servants and not think of ourselves so much. Then God can use us.

I think one college-age student put it best. He was talking with his school friends, most of who didn't know God personally. He said, "You are all looking to things outside of your control to give you happiness. You are hoping that the great job, new car, wonderful family will all work out—then you'll be happy. I'm different. My life is wrapped up in God. It doesn't matter if I get all those external things. I could be on a deserted island and still be happy because I'd still have God." This student understands the source of significance. Wrap yourself in the person of God, and everything else will pale in comparison.

Decision Points

What false source of significance are you most vulnerable to embracing? Lisa finally was able to wrap herself in the Prince of Peace, her only true source of significance. What trait of God can you wrap yourself in? One way to find verses to wrap around your heart is to list the setbacks, shortcomings, or footholds that may have been in your life. Do you have negative thoughts that plague your thinking and keep you from stepping out into your place in God's plan? List two to three areas that keep tripping you up. Write down antonyms of those words, and then look up verses to memorize that will help rebuild your life from God's point of view.

For example:

I struggle with: Anger
God is: Peace, calm, love
I struggle with: Fear, anxiety, stress
God is: Confidence, strength, all-knowing, all-powerful, able

Now look up verses that contain key words that follow your "God is." (A concordance will help.) Choose several verses that encourage your heart. String them together to form a paragraph or two that you can memorize and reflect on when you feel vulnerable to false sources of significance. For example, if I struggle with feeling inadequate, being frozen by fear, or feeling overwhelmed, I might string together some verses.[3] Then I could personalize the verses and paraphrase them as if God is speaking directly to me:

Praise be to You, O Lord, God of our father Israel, from everlasting to everlasting. Yours, O Lord, is the greatness and the power and the glory and the majesty and the splendor, for everything in heaven and earth is Yours. Yours, O Lord, is the kingdom; You are exalted as head over all. Wealth and honor come from You; You are the ruler of all things. In Your hands are strength and power to exalt and give strength to all, even me. Now, our God, I give You thanks and praise Your glorious name. You, Lord, are my strength and my shield; my heart trusts in You, and I am helped. You will not let my foot slip. I know whom I have believed, and am convinced that You are able to guard what I have entrusted to You for that day. You have called me and You are faithful and You will do it. For no matter how many promises You have made, they are "Yes" in Christ.

I have a favorite verse that describes what happens when we trade in our fears and weaknesses for God's strengths and character. Isaiah 61:3 says God will provide:

> A crown of beauty instead of ashes, the oil of gladness instead of mourning, and a garment of praise instead of a spirit of despair. They will be called oaks of righteousness, a planting of the Lord for the display of his splendor.

Decide you want to be authentic. Be the best you that God intended, and trade in the ashes of false sources of significance for the real deal. God's power will work through you because of your relationship with Him. Isaiah 61:3 states the outcome: a life filled with gladness, beauty, and positive praise so that when people see your strength of character (like an oak tree), the display is called "splendid!" I know I want a splendid life—how about you? Make your list of weaknesses and fears and trade them in for God's power and plan.

3

Decide to Get Over It

Overcoming Obstacles to Forge a Future

*A*fter pushing yourself on an all-night project, after working year in, year out at the same job, or after making yet another change to an already crazy schedule, have you ever wondered, *Why am I doing this?* Sometimes it might be for honorable reasons: to keep your word, to fulfill a need, to pinch hit for a friend. But sometimes it might be because you've been set up to do it. You've been programmed to stay in a system that isn't working. Our past does affect our future.

I was raised in Oregon. Athena was a small clean town of less than a hundred people, and I was related to many of them. It was just the kind of town that Norman Rockwell might have painted. It was all-American. But even though I grew up in an incredibly loving community, in a home with a beautiful yard and a welcome mat at the door, my life behind the white picket fence wasn't always filled with peace and tranquility.

I was the oldest child, and from my earliest memories of grade school, I remember thinking I had to be perfect to be accepted and to feel loved. I wanted all my papers to be A plus. I wanted to be the best in my dance class, and anything less meant I felt like a failure. Once when I was eight years old, I was taking a ballet class with girls much older than myself, mostly high school students. My teacher happened to correct my posture, and I ran to the bathroom and locked myself in. It took my mom and the teacher nearly an hour to talk me out. It seems to me I was always in tears because I always felt like a failure—even though I was an obedient little girl and a good student. Why would someone so young be so hard on herself?

I think it was because I had a father who loved me deeply and often sacrificed greatly for me, especially financially, but who had pain deep in his heart. He chose to answer that pain with alcohol rather than with a relationship with God. Living with my dad was a Dr. Jekyl-Mr. Hyde experience. Dad would lovingly waltz me around the living room, and then a short time later he would lash out in anger. Whenever he drank, he would change.

Going Back to Move Forward

As I look back on my life, I can see when seeds of perfectionism were planted. Once when I brought home a report card in seventh grade, it read 100%; 100%; 100%; 100%; 100%; 100%; 99.9%. My dad had been drinking, so "Jack Daniel" said through him, "Pam, why isn't that a 100?" I remember wondering if I would ever be good enough to earn his love.

When I was eight, almost nine, the pastor of our small church (which looked like one of those tiny white church banks kids put quarters in on Sundays) asked my Sunday school class if anyone wanted to learn more about Jesus. I remember thinking, *Okay, we get Christmas because of this guy—yeah, I'll raise my hand.* We learned much about who Jesus is, and we also had an opportunity to gain a place on the quiz team. Now, because I always wanted to achieve, I wanted a place on that team! I could just see myself, like a contestant on *Hollywood Squares,* up on that podium and answering those questions. But to gain a spot on the team, I had to memorize Matthew 5, 6, and 7. While reading Matthew, I came across the verse, "For everyone who asks receives, and he who seeks finds, and to him who knocks it shall be opened." I thought, *Does this mean that if I ask You to come into my life, Jesus, You'll do it?*

There, sitting on my bed, I bowed my head and prayed, asking Jesus to come into my life to be my Savior, Lord, and best friend. I believe He met me there that day.

I felt free and loved unconditionally. The next day was Sunday and, as usual, our pastor invited people forward for prayer. I was crying. I remember him asking me, "What's wrong, Pam?" (He did a good job of not rolling his eyes because I was always crying!) I answered him, "I am so happy!"

Soon after that my best friend, Kelly, mentioned a quiet time. I asked, "What is that?" She explained that every day we should read our Bible and pray. So I began to do that. Even though my dad's alcoholism increased, my freedom and joy were not diminished because my significance was being piped in from heaven.

However, after several geographic moves, I found myself reading my Bible less and less and finally not much at all. Those old perfectionist thoughts returned and haunted my teen years. I thought, *Maybe if I get straight A's—then I'll feel loved and accepted. Oh, maybe if I'm chosen to be a cheerleader…yeah that will make me feel loved and accepted. It must be a college scholarship; that will make me feel worthwhile. No, it must be if I date the coolest guy who drives the coolest car, then surely I will feel valuable. If I win homecoming queen, that crown on my head will surely make me feel validated, right?* I worked hard to achieve all those things, and I still felt empty inside! I was definitely looking for love in all the wrong places.

One day I drove home during my freshman year at junior college and found my parents arguing. Because of my dad's drinking problem, the arguments occurred virtually every day. Dad would rage and Mom would try to calm him down. It was late in the evening, so I turned to my younger sister and brother and said, "I don't know about you, but I'm kind of tired of this. Do you want to go for a drive?" In the car I added, "I don't remember much from Sunday school, but it seems like we should pray for Mom and Dad." We parked in the middle of a cornfield and prayed for our parents. Now, I'm not sure what I expected. Did I think that because I prayed somehow Ozzie and Harriet were going to come down from TV land and be our parents? Despite my hopes, as we entered the house we could still hear our parents arguing. Because this was so normal and it was almost midnight at this point, my brother, sister, and I went to bed.

About 3 A.M., we were awakened to the sound of my mother screaming, "Help me! Help me! Someone please help me!" The three of us bolted from our beds looking for her. I know I was thinking, *Oh no! Dad's anger has escalated into violence and Mom needs to be rescued.* We ran through the dark house but couldn't find Mom anywhere. We pushed open closed doors and still no Mom. We just kept hearing her scream, "Help me! Help me! Someone please help me!" Finally Bret, my six-foot brother, bolted through the door to the garage. There was my mom, not in need of rescue, and my dad, who was trying to hang himself with a rope from the rafters.

My brother pulled Dad inside. I pushed my dad onto the sofa and knelt on his chest. I turned to my mother, brother, and sister and said, "I think Dad really needs us to pray now!" We began to pray. Dad calmed a little, but he was still very agitated. I remember thinking, *He looks wild, crazy.* I was scared and trembling.

Then I remembered the Sunday school story about Saul. When he was upset, David would play the harp and it would calm Saul, so I decided we needed to sing. We sang every Sunday school song we could think of: "Jesus Loves the Little Children," "Jesus Loves Me, This I Know." If it came from church, we sang it. Dad calmed a bit more, but he was still quite upset. Finally, I remembered Dad telling us stories of times when he was a kid. He used to go to tent revival meetings while on a combine harvest crew, sometimes to poke fun of the preachers, but he did say he liked the song

"Amazing Grace." So we sang that over and over and over again until the sun finally rose and he passed out.

My mom, brother, and sister were exhausted—as was I. They headed for bed, but I had diving practice at college. I was hoping to find peace and solace in the water. I went to practice and didn't tell anyone about what had happened at my house the night before. Then I drove back home, hoping I would walk into the house and see the family gathered and they would say, "We can't live like this anymore." But as I walked in, I realized my family really didn't want to talk about it—especially my dad, a very successful businessman, who was sitting at the kitchen table, doing his paperwork.

A Change in the System

Nothing had changed in my family that day, but something had changed in me. On that same drive home, God began talking to me—not audibly, but my heart heard the message clearly. "Pam, you have been treating Me like I'm like your earthly father, that I'm somehow distant, demanding, and unrelenting—but I'm not like that! Dust off that Bible. Get to know Me."

So I began to read my Bible again. Soon after my father's suicide attempt, I read in Romans 8:15: "For you did not receive a spirit that makes you a slave again to fear, but you received the Spirit of sonship. And by him we cry, 'Abba, Father.' " I soon found out that as our children say "da-da" when they learn to speak, Jewish children say "Abba-abba." I realized I had a Daddy in heaven who loved me, not for what I could do but simply because He made me. Over the next few years I began to write down everytime I learned something about God being my Father.

As I spent time getting to know God, my freedom returned. Being driven to achieve didn't seem as critical for gaining acceptance, love, or significance. Rather, as I felt loved by God, I felt free to be me. In having Him lead me, I excelled—it seemed without much effort. I studied hard and always fulfilled my promises, but not because I was frantically stressing out to do so. Instead, it just seemed the natural thing to do. Achievement started to become a result rather than fuel for the fire of some desperate search for validation.

Steps to Freedom

I had a choice. I was at a *decision point.* Would I do nothing and set myself up for repeating the same dysfunction my family tree had handed me, or would I let God remake me from the inside out so I could "get over it!" Many people blame their moms and dads for the mistakes, patterns, and dysfunction in their own life, but that can be a cop-out. We all hit a point in time when *our life* becomes *our choice.*

Your heavenly Father loves you and wants to complete a great work in your life no matter where you came from. God knows the great places you can rise to. Philippians 1:6 says, "He who began a good work in you will carry it on to completion until the day of Christ Jesus." One day in a quiet time, I remember God asking me, *Will you look at your dad through My eyes instead of yours?* See, to me, my dad was a no-good alcoholic, but God pointed out to me that he was a man separated from God, and that a symptom of that separation was alcoholism. In looking at my dad in this way, I could distance myself from the tentacles of alcohol's negative messages to me. I began to be able to love Dad again, unconditionally, not because he did things to deserve my love (because he didn't very often), but because he was created by God.

I was freed to learn what healthy love looked like. I had been chasing love, filling my life with men and often dating many at the same time. I wanted to wait until marriage to enjoy my sexuality, but before this point I had been running out of reasons to wait, and pressure from my boyfriend at the time was mounting.

Also, statistics say if you are raised by an alcoholic parent, you will either become an alcoholic or marry one. If you are raised with rage, you become violent or you expect to be treated with violence. I decided that I didn't want to live by statistics but by God's Spirit!

I decided to try life God's way. As I was freed to love by God, I was also freed from the pressure of feeling I had to give away my sexuality in order to gain love. I broke off a relationship that was not honoring God. Also, I quit dating for six months because I wanted to see if I could exist without the identity of being someone's girlfriend. I found out that not only could I exist without dating, I could choose to have standards for those men I would someday date. As God rebuilt my view of myself from His point of view, I gained the bonus of also having Him rebuild my view of love, romance, and marriage.

God continued to remake the warped way my mind thought over the next year. As I looked in my closet one afternoon in my dorm, I thought, *Hmm, I have a date next Friday. I need a new dress, new shoes, and maybe a new trench coat—I think I'll go see Dad.* My dad had a habit of trying to make amends after he had been drinking. He would do or say something hurtful, but then the next day he wouldn't really remember much of what happened (an alcoholic blackout), although he would vaguely remember feeling bad about what had transpired. When he felt bad, he would open up his wallet and pull out some cash or a credit card and try to buy us off, thus easing his conscience. I headed up to visit him, knowing full well he'd drink, knowing he'd feel bad, knowing he'd give me money—and thus I could buy a new outfit. I had begun to plan my life around my dad's guilt.

On that four-hour car trip to Dad's place, God captured my attention. *Pam, do you want to be the kind of woman who manipulates people with their pain and guilt?*

No, Lord. That day I gave up my right to manipulate my dad based on his guilt. This was a *big change.* You see, a few years later Bill and I dated and became engaged. A few days after our engagement, my father, who traveled as a part of his job, was in town and wanted to take Bill and me to dinner. It was a nice dinner. Dad was on his best behavior. He was dressed in a suit, he was sober, and he was actually listening to Bill and me in conversation. Then he said, "Kids, why don't you two come up to Stockton and see me in a few weeks. I'd like to give you some money for the wedding." He named an amount.

A few weeks later, hopeful that this too would be a positive visit with my dad, Bill and I headed up to Stockton. When we arrived at Dad's house, he wasn't there. He had been out water-skiing with his buddies. When Dad water-skied, Dad drank beer. When Dad drank beer, he ended up in a "barbecue" kind of mood. Shortly after he arrived, he threw some meat on the barbecue and continued drinking. Well, when you drink that much beer, what you get when you barbecue is a burnt offering. Dad plopped an unrecognizable piece of meat onto a plate, and when the fork wouldn't even go in, we realized no one could eat it.

I said, "That's okay, Dad. I didn't come to eat your meat. I came to spend time with you. I'll just order some pizza." When the pizza arrived, we sat down at the dining room table. Because my dad had been drinking beer all day, he was sick all over the pizza. I remember throwing myself across my new fiancé trying to spare him from the scene—as if I could do that! I helped my dad to clean himself up and packed him off to bed. I also cleaned up the kitchen, and then I said to Bill, "We need to go to the park and pray. I can tell you that in the morning Dad is going to feel really bad about what has happened. He may not remember exactly what he's done, but he will feel bad. We need to decide right now how much money we would have taken if he would have been sober because I don't want strings of guilt to follow us into our new relationship." As we talked and prayed, we remembered the amount Dad had offered to give us at dinner weeks before when he was sober, and we decided that we would accept no more than that.

Sure enough, the next day Dad woke up feeling really bad. He offered to write a check that would have provided a royal wedding for me. But I knew I didn't want my significance to be built on a false foundation. I would rather have a simple wedding with a pure heart than a fancy one with strings.

Step-by-step, God was asking me: *Will you forgive your dad? Trust Me, as you forgive, you will gain freedom.* I forgave, and as I did I gained the freedom to move away from false significance and toward true significance given by God.

Wounded Healers

Bill and I have enjoyed the benefit of having Jim and Sally Conway as wonderful mentors in the faith and in ministry. Jim once told Bill, "We are all wounded healers." I have seen that is true. The more I allow God to redeem my dark side, the more freedom I experience and the more I am free to be used by God. Sam Rima and Gary McIntosh, in their book *Overcoming the Dark Side of Leadership*, describe the importance of allowing God to redeem back the hurts and rebuild our lives with His love:

> It was during this research that it became clear that a paradox of sorts existed in the lives of most of the leaders who had experienced significant failures: The personal insecurities, feelings of inferiority, and need for parental approval (among other dysfunctions) that compelled these people to become successful leaders were very often the same issues that precipitated their failure.[1]

It seems God takes our God-given personality and giftedness and, if we are willing, redeems back our inferiorities, mistakes, and hurts to shape us into the people He wants us to be.

> Most often their ambition has been a subtle and dangerous combination of their own dysfunctional personal needs and a certain measure of their altruistic desire to expand the kingdom of God. However, because ambition is so easily disguised in Christian circles and couched in spiritual language (the need to fulfill the great commission and expand the church), the dysfunctions that drive Christian leaders often go undetected and unchallenged until it is too late.[2]

So You're Not Perfect

I believe God gives us opportunities to deal with these dysfunctional foundations of significance if we are aware of them. If I embrace my imperfections, I can be free to be a woman God can use. When I did my quiet times of all the "You Ares" God says about us, I was very encouraged by many of the positive ones: you are strong, chosen, children of the promise, standing firm, and so on. But for me personally, the ones that were most freeing were the ones that at first appeared negative. Some of these I didn't like, and I wished they weren't even there! For example, 1 Corinthians 3:2-4 explains, "You are still not ready. You are still worldly." Romans 6:19 says, "You are weak in your natural selves." Hebrews 5:11 mentions that we are "slow to learn."

I came to realize that freedom isn't the same as denial. I am still worldly, I am weak, I am slow to learn, and if I ever think I have arrived, I will be lying to myself. These things are just as true about me—and you—as all the other more positive things God says about who we are. Jesus has done us a favor when He tells us in Matthew

15:19: "For out of the heart proceed evil thoughts, murders, adul-
teries, fornications, thefts, false witness, blasphemies" (NKJV). It is
to our advantage to recognize that we have a bent towards self-
ishly wanting our way over God's way. And every time we give into
our selfishness we prove: "There is no one righteous, not even one;
there is no one who understands, no one who seeks God. All have
turned away, they have together become worthless; there is no one
who does good, not even one" (Romans 3:10-12).

God knows we don't always have it all together. But we have
this encouragement from the apostle Paul: "When I am weak, then
I am strong" (2 Corinthians 12:10). Yes, we may be weak in our
natural selves, but Paul doesn't leave us there in Romans 6:19. In
verse 22 he says, "Now that you have been set free from sin and
have become slaves to God, the benefit you reap leads to holiness,
and the result is eternal life."

How does this transformation take place? Romans 3:24 says
that we "are justified freely by his grace." Justification is a legal
term. It is a picture of all our sins being logged into a portfolio
or file. (And each of us has a thick file of imperfections, mistakes,
and sins! Think of it as your permanent record or, as those in law
enforcement call it, your "jacket.") Then God sent His Son, Jesus,
down to earth to live a sinless life. He had a file folder full of perfect
credits. On the cross, God took our sins from our file and switched
them with Jesus' righteousness. Jesus paid the penalty for our file
folders—for our jackets of imperfections! God now looks down
on us from heaven and sees Christ's righteousness where our sins
once were.

Justification is a one-time act that happens when we meet
Christ. Having justified us, God begins a process of sanctification.
Second Corinthians 3:17-18 tells us: "Now the Lord is the Spirit,
and where the Spirit of the Lord is, there is freedom. And we, who
with unveiled faces all reflect the Lord's glory, are being transformed into his likeness with ever-increasing glory, which comes

from the Lord, who is the Spirit." Jesus is in the process of moving us from the weakness that characterized our lives before conversion up toward our position of strength as seen from heaven. He's renewing and rebuilding us. It is only as we continue to acknowledge our imperfections that He transforms them. I love the prayer in Psalm 139:23-24: "Search me, O God, and know my heart; test me and know my anxious thoughts. See if there is any offensive way in me, and lead me in the way everlasting."

Playing a New CD

After seminary Bill and I headed to youth ministry. One of the challenges was needing to staff the junior high, high school, and college-age classes all at the same time on Sunday morning. I volunteered for the junior high group, which quickly grew from a handful to about 70 kids. But as the group grew, being junior highers, they became more and more of a challenge to control— and I do mean *control*. Because that's what I tried to do. Teaching was secondary to keeping them in order. One day I actually thought I was going to lose it. I felt anger rising to the surface, and it was going to erupt like Mount Vesuvius all over those kids.

So I prayed! *Help me, Jesus.* And He did! That day, I realized, they were just being junior highers and it was *my* problem, not theirs, that God wanted to work on. I was a control freak, and I could almost hear God say, "Pam, there's one God, and you're not it!"

I had seen my controlling behavior in a variety of smaller issues in my life and relationships. I knew that because I had grown up in a home that was out of control, I could easily become a controller. I had to replace the old CD message that programmed me with a need to control with a new CD that reminded me that only God is in control. I began to ask God to redeem this part of my personality.

The first step was to forgive my dad for producing this trait. As I forgave and yielded, I experienced growth. God is working every day to whittle down the control freak in me!

This same anger has another ugly head. It used to be that when stress or strenuous circumstances hit my life, anger was the first emotion that rose to the surface. Often, this anger would be taken out on Bill, undeservedly so. One day as I was ranting, Bill walked over, wrapped his arms around me (he had to or my flailing arms could have hurt him!), and he said, "Pam, what are you really feeling? Are you really this angry with me, or could it be something deeper?" He was right; I had a deep-seated fear of failure! Again, I forgave Dad for planting the seed and asked God to redeem it. Now when I am feeling that same stress and anger rising to the surface, I ask God to help me communicate my insecurities rather than become angry. I will say something similar to, "Hey, I need to share something with you. I'm feeling like I might fail here, which causes me to have some strong emotions inside. Can we stop and pray and then brainstorm a way to alleviate this fear?" Now the hysterics, fireworks, and rantings I experienced years ago rarely appear. I am freer every day as a new CD plays in my heart and head.

Bill and I have experienced much freedom in forgiveness, and we find that we use it in all of our counseling. There are six basic principles, and if a person can walk their way through these six statements, they gain a handle on how to forgive in a tangible way.

Forgiveness says:

1. I forgive (person) for (offense).

2. I admit that what was done was wrong.

3. I do not expect (person) to make up for what he has done.

4. I will not use this offense to define who (person) is.

5. I will not manipulate (person) with the offense.

6. I will not allow the offense to stop my growth.

These are all principles taken from what Jesus did on the cross for us. He knew our sins—each and every one of them—and He died for them. But to receive the benefit of Christ's death on the cross, we have to admit we are wrong. We have to repent. God didn't expect us to make up for our sins. He knew we couldn't—it is impossible. God doesn't define us by our sin; rather, He defines us from His point of view. He doesn't manipulate us with all He knows about us, and He doesn't allow our imperfections to keep us from Him. Instead, He allows us to partner with Him for our growth.

Why Am I Doing This?

God knew that I needed to continue to allow Him to redeem my dark side. While spending time with Jim and Sally Conway, Jim told me, "Pam, people who have been wounded, like us, from homes like ours, often make decisions based on our sickness, not health. It is as if you have a tube inside you. You receive a compliment, and it feels so good going down. But the bad thing is it is a bottomless tube, so the positive praise goes right out the bottom. We constantly need more praise. We easily fall into the trap of making our decisions based upon what will bring us the most praise, the most public applause, the greatest possibility for compliments. But because the tube is bottomless, it is self-defeating. You can't fill the tube."

I responded back to Jim, "As Solomon says in the book of Ecclesiastes, vanity of vanities, all is vanity. No amount of praise will do it, so I need a different standard of decision making, right?" I knew I had always struggled with pleasing people, even if in doing so I was caused distress. I would always seek to alleviate others' stress—especially when it would result in praise of any kind.

"Right," said Jim, "because our wounds make us vulnerable to praise, we can be easily manipulated and sell ourselves to anyone or anything, just to get some affirmation."

"Like selling our birthright for a pot of stew?" I asked, smiling. I knew exactly what Jim was talking about. I had been aware of this "tube" in me for a while. It was only my quiet times and God daily centering me that kept me from chasing praise with a get-it-at-all-costs attitude. My daily time with God helped me to step out in obedience instead of just staying in my safety zone where I would be assured of successes and praise. As my writing and speaking grew, God prepared me for this next step by reminding me to "guard the gift" He had placed in me. He helped me think my way through business decisions, rather than just going by feelings, which I was vulnerable to doing. Sometimes "thinking" instead of "feeling" feels risky.

In risking I actually receive affirmation because I am growing as a person. But it can be a scary place emotionally because with each risk there is no guarantee of success or praise. In fact, in risking people's worlds are often shaken up, causing criticism to sometimes come your way. I had chosen years before to get off the merry-go-round of trying to please everyone—I knew I couldn't. I had tried and tried to please my dad, and I rarely heard him verbally praise me. I had seen that as I tried to please everyone in ministry, or life, for that matter, I felt like a chicken with her head cut off, frantically running around. Trying to please created a lot of activity but not many results. So I began to ask myself before any decision, "Why am I doing this?" Then I'd run down the checklist: To receive praise? To try to be perfect? To try to control people or circumstances? Are my motives pure on this one? The closer I watch over my motives, the more I am able to enjoy the journey and not worry as much about the outcome. The words of Galatians 6:14 are etched on my heart. "May I never boast except in the cross of our Lord Jesus Christ, through which the world has been crucified to me, and I to the world."

For years, I have trained myself to mentally flip my heart to that page of my mind anytime I receive praise. It catalogs the compliment where it should be, under "C" for Christ. By doing this, I am able to appreciate the person giving the compliment and encouragement, and I am able to focus my heart on Christ and all He has done for me. I am also able to carry any kind of responsibility God sends my way because nothing is "too big" or "too small." It's all just a calling. You have yours, I have mine. God can use us when we are not worried about who gets the credit. Anything He asks is a wonderful opportunity—because He is doing the asking.

Overcome Evil with Good

God used one more step with my dad to free my motives and thus free me to make clearer decisions. God kept prodding me to bless my dad. First it started small. I set up all decisions about my dad with one question: "What would a loving daughter do in a healthy father-daughter relationship?" Then I'd set boundaries to move our relationship toward health (for example, not talking with Dad late at night when he was drunk but calling him in the morning when he was sober), and I'd have my gestures of love toward him be the same as a loving daughter regardless of how he acted toward me (for example, Dad rarely sent me a birthday gift or card, but I always sent him one).

A few years ago, God began to prod me to write a blessing to my dad. I had learned over the years that my father had never heard the words "I love you" from his own alcoholic father. I learned that he had grown up dirt poor, so he also had a huge fear of failure that drove him to workaholism. I never made excuses for Dad, but I did seek to try to understand him, and I sought to keep seeing him from God's point of view. A few years ago, at

Christmas, I knew it was time to write the blessing. But where do you start when you have so many painful memories and so few good ones? I prayed. *God, help me write something to Dad so that he will know I love him—but more importantly, that You love him. Let him see that Your love can absorb his pain.*

As I wrote the tribute I could see how some of my best traits were ones God had redeemed out of darkness into the light. Because I grew up never knowing when Dad would rage, it was as if I lived my life on alert. Because I've allowed God to redeem that fear, it turned into a God-given ability to read people, to sense how they are feeling. I can read between people's emotional lines. Because I grew up mediating between Dad and everyone in our family, I have the ability to mediate now, which is a handy skill for a leader! But my favorite trait that God redeemed is the one I wrote about in my tribute to Dad.

On Christmas Day, I stood and read this tribute face-to-face to my father:

Our Golden Treasure

It was a sunny Saturday morning. Excited children piled out of cars, baskets in hand. It was the day before Easter, the day of our small town's big egg hunt. I was nervous and excited, as were all the other preschoolers. I held tight to my dad's hand. The whistle blew, and the race to find the prized golden egg was on! I picked up a pink egg and then a green one, and I placed them gently in my basket. But what I really wanted was that golden egg. The hunt seemed as though it lasted a lifetime. It seemed that no one could find the golden egg.

Dad said, "Come here, honey."

He bent down and whispered into my ear and pointed at the ground. I looked down at a disgusting sight—an egg smashed and broken from being trampled upon by tiny feet.

"But it's broken!" I said to my dad.

"What color is it, Charlie?"

I shrugged my shoulders.

"Look close. What color do you see?"

I tried hard to find a piece of shell big enough to discern its color. I picked up a small fragment and yelled, "It's gold! Daddy, it's gold!" But how was I supposed to get it over to the judges?

"Pick it up. Moms and dads can't touch the prized egg. You have to carry it."

"Ick! It's too yucky, Daddy! I can't."

"If you want the prize, you have to pick it up. But I will help you carry it."

We bent down and I scooped up as much of the egg remnant as my tiny hands could carry. It felt awful. Dad slid his hand under mine, and together we carried our broken treasure to the judges. I was awarded a huge basket brimming with Easter goodies. Dad was proud of me, and I was proud of him.

In the years since, I have often thought of that day. It is a picture of our father-daughter relationship. My dad is a lot like that broken golden egg. He has often felt inadequate to be all that he wanted to be as a dad. His heart is like that egg—full of prizewinning potential but cracked by the heartache of broken dreams. Dad has a heart of gold, but it often goes unseen by those around him. Words fail him. Sometimes his actions fall short of the feelings he'd like to express. But I've always held on to a piece of that prizewinning potential, just like I held on to that small piece of golden shell. I've held on to the golden moments that Dad and I have shared. Like that day in the park, when I was proud of him and he was proud of me. And when times are hard, I sometimes hear that whisper, "If you want the prize, you have to pick it up." So I gather up the pieces of life and carry what life requires me to carry.

No, Dad is not perfect, but neither am I. So I hold tight to that less-than-perfect treasure because all that has happened—the good and the bad—God has used to make me the woman I've wanted to be. I have become a woman who can look at a bad situation, find the gold in it, and go on.

I'm a prizewinner in my daddy's eyes, and his love is a golden treasure to me.

After I read it, Dad said, tears rolling down his cheeks, "Charlie, thanks. Thanks for using your writing to say such nice things about this bad ol', good ol' boy. If you ever want to use my story to help other people, go right ahead." That was the first time I ever remember Dad complimenting my writing—and the best part was that I didn't *need* it. I could receive it and enjoy it, but I didn't need it. I wasn't frantic for approval because I had already heard the applause from my heavenly Father. Listen, can you hear it? Your applause, too, is from on high.

Decision Points

Make a list of some of the negative traits that could have been trained into you while growing up. How could these be affecting your decision-making skills today? Take a step to replace the old CD with a new one. Try one of these activities:

1. Make a list of people and events that you need to forgive. Then pray your way through the six statements of forgiveness on pages 61-62.

2. Pray that God would make you aware of any old CDs that need to be replaced with new messages from His Book.

3. Write a blessing or tribute to someone who has wounded you. In it include how God turned pain into something positive.

4. Make a list of reasons to "get over it." At 19 I decided I didn't want to marry an alcoholic or a violent man. I didn't want children who lived in fear in their own home. I wanted a life-long happy marriage and kids who were successful because they had confidence in God and in themselves, not worka-holics who achieved because they feared failure. Now, almost 25 years later and with two children out of the nest, I can say I have those dreams. The dysfunction stopped with a series of decisions to do life God's way. Doing life God's way may seem hard, but repeating dysfunction is harder still. Make a list of motivating factors—a list of dreams and goals—that will help you to keep deciding to decide to do life God's way.

Decide to Turn Up the Truth

Turn Down the Negative and Turn to the Positive

I love greeting cards. They carry such encouraging messages, especially at Christmas. I post the cards around the archway between my living room and my dining room because they are so beautiful to look at. But however beautiful the card, or however encouraging the message, the card couldn't arrive at my home without the envelope it came in.

I always try to pray with the leadership teams at the churches I speak in prior to going to the platform. While in Missouri, one of the women prayed, "Thank You, Lord, for the message Pam is about to deliver to our hearts. Thank You that she is an envelope for Your message of hope and encouragement."

I thought, *Yes! I love it! I am simply an envelope! He is the message; I just have to carry it.*

The more I thought about that analogy, the more I liked it. There are all kinds of envelopes. Some envelopes are bright and colorful, like many cute and perky women. Some are professional and functional, like letterhead. Others are more elaborate, the kind of envelope you might pick up at a stationery store for invitations. Other envelopes are functional manila gals, but these are often entrusted with some very important messages. Others of us look like a plain envelope on the outside, but when you open us up, you can see that we are lined with the gold leaf foil of wedding invitations. Then some of us are like FedEx packages—we do things very, very fast. Just like envelopes, women come in all shapes, colors, and sizes, but we are all still envelopes. There is no Envelope Hall of Fame and no envelope IQ test. Every envelope is important because we all carry the message of the hope, freedom, peace, and joy found in a personal relationship with God.

Signed, Sealed, and Delivered

In 2 Corinthians 3:2-3, the apostle Paul says, "You yourselves are our letter, written on our hearts, known and read by everybody. You show that you are a letter from Christ, the result of our ministry, written not with ink but with the Spirit of the Living God, not on tablets of stone but on tablets of human hearts." *You are a letter.*

Everyday, in every way, believers' lives are being read by others. Age isn't a factor in our worth to God, and we've already discussed that size, shape, color, and speed aren't factors, either. We're all envelopes carrying a valuable, needed message to the world where we live. We are valuable not because of our outward packaging but because we carry a valuable message. We've been chosen to carry the message of hope.

It's so easy to forget the freedom we have in being God's envelope. One of the things that are a part of my life as a writer is media appearances. Bill and I have our own radio program, but quite often our publishers also have us appear as guests on other radio and television programs. One year Bill and I were to appear on a national television talk show. As with all television appearances, each guest takes a turn in the makeup chair. This is never my favorite part because I struggle with acne. I've been under a doctor's care for it since I was 16. I once asked a dermatologist, "I'm almost 30, and my face still thinks I'm 17! When will this stop?" He asked about some family history, and then he said, "Mrs. Farrel, it may never stop. It sounds like it is hereditary in your family." Oh, great news!

I often tease that I have the perfect face for *radio!* Anyway, I sat down in this makeup artist's chair, and she said as she stared into the mirror, "You don't have a happy face."

"Actually, I am very excited about today. This is a wonderful opportunity." Then I smiled.

"No, you do not have a happy face." Now at this point, I knew she was talking about my skin. She began the usual battery of questions and suggestions all the while reminding me that I didn't have a "happy face." Well, inside I felt emotions rising, but I didn't want to cry because then I'd have to sit even longer and have my makeup redone! When she was called by the star of the show into the next room for a brief moment, I looked at my not so "happy" face in the mirror.

Lord, this is really hard to hear. It's doing nothing for my confidence. Please help me get my focus off my not so "happy" face! Okay, God, why did I come? To show my face to 60 million viewers? No. I have Your message to deliver. This is not about me, it's about You. It's about Your message. Then I looked at my face again. *Lord, I think I look pretty good for an envelope!*

I knew God had chosen me for this task. I was chosen to be His envelope that day. And deliver His message I did!

Return to Sender

Because Jesus chooses whom to send when and where, we can be free from some of the insecurities that hold us back. In one of my Women of Influence talks, I ask the audience to share what they think holds women back. Everywhere I travel the same things are mentioned: Women feel they are not smart enough, trained enough, or eloquent enough. They feel they might be rejected. They are afraid that others may say, "Who does she think she is?" or "I don't want to be her friend."

Sometimes women feel inadequate and overwhelmed. We're not sure how we could do one more thing. Thomas Edison said,

"Opportunity is missed by most people because it is dressed up in overalls and looks like work." Some of us don't want more work!

A few of us feel men are holding us back. However, most of us believe in the ability of women to find a way to make a difference. Faith Whittlesey said, "Remember, Ginger Rogers did everything Fred Astaire did, but she did it backward and in high heels."

However, the number one, most common thing my audiences mention is fear of failure.

Why do we fear failure? In it we often find the strands of future success. Here are some reflections about failure from people others have called a success:

Medical doctor, Scottish author, and social reformer Samuel Smiles said, "It is a mistake to suppose that men succeed through success; they much oftener succeed through failures. Precept, study, advice, and example could never have taught them so well as failure has done."

Businessman Thomas J. Watson agreed, "Would you like me to give you a formula for success? It's quite simple, really. Double your rate of failure. You are thinking of failure as the enemy of success. But it isn't at all. You can be discouraged by failure—or you can learn from it. So go ahead and make mistakes. Make all you can. Because, remember, that's where you will find success."

W.E. Gladstone, a four-term prime minister of England wrote, "No man ever becomes great or good except through many and great mistakes."

Writer Orison Swett Marden noted, "You cannot measure a man by his failures. You must know what use he makes of them. What did they mean to him? What did he get out of them?"

Joseph Sugarman, a leader in the marketing industry said, "Not many people are willing to give failure a second opportunity. They fail once and it is all over. The bitter pill of failure is often more than most people can handle. If you are willing to accept failure and learn from it, if you are willing to consider failure as a blessing in disguise and bounce back, you have got the essential of harnessing one of the most powerful success forces." H.L. Wayland continued that thought with, "Show us a man who never makes a mistake, and we will show you a man who never makes anything. The capacity for occasional blundering is inseparable from the capacity to bring things to pass. The only men who are past the danger of making mistakes are the men who sleep at Greenwood [cemetery]."[1]

"If you don't accept failure as a possibility, you don't set high goals, and you don't branch out, you don't try—you don't take the risk," said First Lady Rosalynn Carter.

Politicians grapple with the possibility of eminent failure, and it is that daily stare down with failure that propels them into greater leadership. Prime Minister Sir Winston Churchill said, "Success is the ability to go from failure to failure without losing your enthusiasm." Legislator S.I. Hayakawa concurred, "Notice the difference between when a man says to himself, 'I have failed three times' and what happens when he says, 'I'm a failure.'" President Theodore Roosevelt echoes the need for a positive outlook on failure, "Far better it is to dare mighty things, to win glorious triumphs, even though checkered by failure, than to take rank with those poor spirits who neither enjoy much nor suffer much because they live in the gray twilight that knows not victory nor defeat."

Failure isn't final. Motivational speaker Dennis Witley said, "Failure should be our teacher, not our undertaker. Failure is delay, not defeat. It is a temporary detour, not a dead end. Failure is something we can avoid only by saying nothing, doing nothing, and being nothing." Film actress Mary Pickford declared, "Failure is not the falling down, but the staying down." Inventor and automobile manufacturer Henry Ford said, "Failure is simply the opportunity to begin again, this time more intelligently."

Warren Bennis, author, educator, and sociologist at the University of Southern California, said, "The leaders I met, whatever walk of life they were from, whatever institutions they were presiding over, always referred back to the same failure, something that happened to them that was personally difficult, even traumatic, something that made them feel that desperate sense of hitting bottom—a something they thought was almost a necessity. It's as if at that moment the iron entered their soul; that moment created the resilience that leaders need."[2]

Failure does place iron within our soul. Even small failures help mold us into women God can use. In the ninth grade I was ranked number one in the state in gymnastics. I had won all the district and regional meets, and all I needed to do was to show up at the state meet, do what I had been doing all year, and then I'd win. Things were going well until I rotated to the vaulting event. It was my strongest event. I had a good vault with a higher technical merit than almost every one at the meet. I ran like a steaming locomotive down the runway. I hit the board that was to launch me up and over the vault to a gold medal—and instead I heard and felt a CRASH! I had run straight into the vaulting horse. I felt dazed, stunned, and breathless. I heard the crowd hush. I slowly picked myself up off the floor. I was in shock. I had never missed a vault in competition. I rarely missed a vault in practice.

I walked back to the end of the runway, shaking my arms and legs to loosen them up and to regain some composure. My coach gave me a few words of encouragement. I prayed, *Oh, Lord, help me!* I raised my arm high over my head to signal the judges that I was ready, gave a quick hop, and then power ran down the blue strip of carpet intent on making a vault and making it stick. CRASH! I'd done the same exact thing—twice. Not only did I fail once in front of the full gym of spectators, I failed twice! A scratch. No score. My dream of being the state champion was gone.

In that moment, I had to decide how to face failure. Would I run crying from the gym and skip my last event because I couldn't win anyway, or would I rise and act like a champion, even if the gold medal would never hang around my neck? I had already lost once when I failed to make the vault, but if I let my emotions win out, I would lose again. If I quit, I'd lose my positive personality and my hope, and because I was the team captain, those following me would lose hope too. Blinking back tears, I rose. I bowed to the judges as if I had just landed a perfect vault, and then I pulled my shoulders back and marched off the floor to the waiting and welcoming arms of my mother and coach.

I let the tears flow as they embraced me, but then I wiped them away while my coach prepared me for my final event, the floor exercise. I didn't stand on the winners dais that afternoon; instead I was handed a fourth-place all-around ribbon. Instead of pouting I chose to shake the hand and hug my teammate who had captured the gold instead of me. She had placed second under me all season, and this was her moment in the sun. My sister, in a lower age division, stood in the first place spot and accepted roses and her medal. Then we had a five-hour trip home. I could choose to make everyone miserable with my attitude or I could choose to be happy for my sister. I had a choice as to my perspective. The truth was that this was one meet. I lost a gold medal, but I didn't lose my health, my life, or a family member. World peace didn't hinge on my performance. Reality check: My ego was bruised, but life was still full of promise and potential. *Pam, pull yourself together, and go "rejoice with those who rejoice!"* (Romans 12:15). That day I learned that *if you act like a champion*, even if the outside world doesn't reward your efforts, *you still feel like a champion* inside.

The Heart of a Champion

Educator Edward Dowden said, "Sometimes a noble failure serves the world as faithfully as a distinguished success." How we fail determines our ability to find and stay in our place in God's plan. God's Word reminds us, "Humble yourselves, therefore, under God's mighty hand, that he may lift you up in due time" (1 Peter 5:6).

I believe God will be faithful to allow you to hear His voice and answer His call. He cares more about you walking in His will than you do! But the trick is *staying* in that place and tenaciously serving there, no matter the trial. *It's not the getting in—it's the staying in that is important.* It is easy, when failure comes in like a tornado, to sneak out the back door, to say, "I've survived one storm. I'm not staying around for another!" But if we really believe God's Word, then we are just where God wants us to be when we are humbled by a failure. We are usable, moldable, listening, and ready to be elevated.

Christiana Tsai could have felt like a failure at one time. Born to a vice governor in a Chinese province, Christiana was educated by Buddhist monks but soon outgrew their knowledge, so she enrolled in a Christian mission school, vowing to never become a Christian. She said, "I made up my mind that I was not going to 'eat' their Christianity, so I used to take a Chinese novel with me to chapel…"[3]

Christiana and a friend, Miss Wu, began to write a book denouncing Christianity. However, Christiana began to read the Bible and listen to preaching in English to improve her skills. "God used my love for English to draw me to Himself."[4] Soon Miss Wu also came to faith in Christ. Success, right? Not everyone thought so.

Christiana shared her new faith with her family. She was bitterly rebuked for disgracing the family name. One brother grabbed her Bible and her hymnbook and tore them to pieces. Her mother was devastated to have a Christian daughter. But Christiana hung in there. She didn't let immediate failure detour her faith. She kept living the life of faith before her friends and family. One by one they slowly responded. Her mother came to faith in Christ and quit a lifelong habit of smoking opium. That change sparked interest in other family members. Mom, two sons, and their wives were baptized. Mom opened up her home for Bible studies, and at age 62 she learned to read so she could read the Bible for herself.

Christiana began teaching in a government school. During class breaks she talked personally with the students, and she opened her home up so that interested students could come and talk about Jesus. Seventy-two of her 200 students came to know Christ. Again, there was outrage. Parents were up in arms! A newspaper article was published claiming the teacher made her students cry, "God! God!" The school's director, Miss Plum, searched the school and confiscated Bibles and threatened expulsion to students caught attending Bible studies. However, the faith of the students withstood the persecution and soon Miss Plum herself came to faith in Christ.

Christiana recorded her journey: "So the brother who tore up my Bible and persecuted me in the early days at last confessed my Lord. In all, fifty-five of my relatives, adults and children, have become God's children...I have never been to college, or theological seminary, and I am not a Bible teacher; I have only been God's 'hunting dog.' I simply followed at the heels of my Master, and brought to His feet the quarry He sent me after."[5]

Because God is the one choosing us, when we obey, we will never be a failure—no matter what the results are. I think we often forget how carefully He chooses and how well He knows us.

He Knows Us

J.I. Packer, in his classic bestselling book *Knowing God*, said it best:

> There is tremendous relief in knowing that His love for me is utterly realistic, based at every point on prior knowledge of the worst about me, so that no discovery can now

disillusion Him about me, in a way which I am so often disillusioned about myself...There is, certainly, great cause for humility in the thought that He sees all the twisted things about me that my fellow men do not see (and I am glad!), and that He sees more corruption in me than that which I see in myself (which, in all conscience, is enough). There is, however, equally great incentive to worship and love God in the thought that, for some unfathomable reason, He wants me as His friend, and desires to be my friend, and has given His Son to die for me in order to realize this purpose. We cannot work these thoughts out here, but merely mentioning them is enough to show how much it means to know, not merely that we know God, but that He knows us.[6]

God knows me. He knows all about me. He knows the good and the bad. He knows every hair on my head and every thought on my mind. He knows my successes and my limitations. He knows I am utterly imperfect. He knows yet He still chooses me. He knows yet He still chooses you. He says: *You are chosen.*

But you are a chosen people, a royal priesthood, a holy nation, a people belonging to God, that you may declare the praises of him who called you out of darkness into his wonderful light. Once you were not a people, but now you are the people of God; once you had not received mercy, but now you have received mercy (1 Peter 2:9-10).

His Choosing

When God says we are chosen, He means we are elected—and He's the only one voting! So when we are all preoccupied about what other people think and say about us, we are forgetting that public opinion doesn't supercede God's appointment.

Not only are you chosen, but you are chosen for royalty. The connotation of this verse is that we are a part of the King's court. We dwell in His palace, and as a royal priesthood we are given a share in reigning with Christ. And when we belong to God, we are preserved for Him and by Him.

Because I am chosen, royal, and preserved by God, I trust Him to be my protection from criticism. I like to picture God as my flak jacket! As I seek to step into my royal role of declaring His praises, I know I will receive some praise and some criticism. The Bible is very clear that in this world I will have tribulation—but it is also clear that Jesus says, "I have overcome the world" (John 16:33). My goal is to grasp what it means to be chosen and royal, and God's commitment is the preservation of my person, regardless of the outcome of my position.

Whenever I grasp the understanding of this picture of who God says I am, I am freer to live life the way it was meant to be. From previous chapters, you know that I started out in life not very confident, always wondering if I would ever be good enough to gain acceptance and love. My fears could have grown in intensity over the years until they paralyzed me in life. Many people live lives filled with fears that hold them back from excelling and stepping into their potential.

A few years ago, my father died. I decided I needed to visit a counselor who specializes in working with those in positions of responsibility and high visibility. He also works well with those who are grieving. Because many people depend on me, I wanted to make sure I worked through my grief in a positive, constructive manner. My counselor gave me a diagnostic test to enumerate the personal strengths and weaknesses of my life. When I got the results back, I was amazed at one of the variables. The test rated a variety of areas, including confidence and a person's ability to see the positive and move forward to achieve positive results in life. The average person usually falls somewhere in the thirtieth percentile—I rated 100 percent! Now I think this is a "God thing"! Only God could change a timid little girl who longed for approval into a woman who is confident in her choices and the way she relates to people and life. I believe as I have embraced the fact that I am chosen it has boosted my confidence.

I love the picture in the next part of the verse, "who called you out of darkness, into his wonderful light." Of course I was called out of darkness! Princesses don't live in dark damp hovels. They live and walk in the light. When apathy and lack of integrity are tempting me to cut corners, I am moving back into the shadows and away from the light I was called to.

When we were in youth ministry, Bill ran a who-can-bring-me-the-biggest-cockroach contest. We had kids bringing us roaches two to four inches long! Each student told a similar story. They had to move quickly to catch their roach because roaches love the dark, and the moment you flip on the light they are running for the shadows. We are not roaches. We weren't made for the dark; we were made for the light. If you find yourself more comfortable hanging out with people who love the darkness rather than the light, or if you can't honestly share what you've been doing, watching, and reading with other princesses of the light, then you have moved from your place in God's plan. I sometimes think we ask the wrong questions of ourselves. Instead of asking, "Is this good enough?" and "Can I skate by with this?" we should be asking, "Am I acting like a benevolent princess?" "Am I pursuing God's light in this area?" God has proclaimed we are already "good enough" because we are chosen, royal envelopes! Our job is to take God at His word and act out our position.

We do have a choice because "once you had not received mercy, but now you have received mercy." There must be a point in time when we choose to walk into the light from out of the darkness. There is a moment when we accept His choosing and His appointing us as royals. There is a point in time we become envelopes carrying His message of hope.

What is that message? What is that choice?

God's Statement of Love to Us

I love you and have a plan for you.

"I came to give life—life in all its fullness" (John 10:10).[7]

"I came so they can have real and eternal life, more and better life than they ever dreamed of" (John 10:10 THE MESSAGE).

"God loved the world so much that he gave his only Son. God gave his Son so that whoever believes in him may not be lost, but have eternal life" (John 3:16).

Because you are imperfect, you are separated from My love and our relationship is broken.

"All people have sinned and are not good enough for God's glory" (Romans 3:23).

"We've compiled this long and sorry record as sinners...and proved that we are utterly incapable of living the glorious lives God wills for us..." (Romans 3:23 THE MESSAGE).

"And when a person knows the right thing to do, but does not do it, then he is sinning" (James 4:17).

"It is your evil that has separated you from your God. Your sins cause him to turn away from you..." (Isaiah 59:2).

Because I love you, I, who am perfect, paid the price for your imperfection so I could restore our relationship.

"But Christ died for us while we were still sinners. In this way God shows his great love for us. We have been made right with

God by the blood of Christ's death. So through Christ we will surely be saved from God's anger. I mean that while we were God's enemies, God made friends with us through the death of his Son. Surely, now we are God's friends, God will save us through his Son's life" (Romans 5:8-10).

"Christ had no sin. But God made him become sin. God did this for us so that in Christ we could become right with God" (2 Corinthians 5:21).

"Christ himself died for you. And that one death paid for your sins. He was not guilty, but he died for those who are guilty. He did this to bring you all to God" (1 Peter 3:18).

"The greatest love a person can show is to die for his friends" (John 15:13).

To initiate this new relationship, all you need to do is accept My payment for your imperfection. I cannot make you love Me. That is your choice.

"I mean that you have been saved by grace because you believe. You did not save yourselves. It was a gift from God. You cannot brag that you are saved by the work you have done. God has made us what we are. In Christ Jesus, God made us new people..." (Ephesians 2:8-10).

"If you use your mouth to say, 'Jesus is Lord,' and if you believe in your heart that God raised Jesus from death, then you will be saved" (Romans 10:9).

"And this is eternal life: that men can know you, the only true God, and that men can know Jesus Christ, the One you sent" (John 17:3).

To accept God's love for you, talk to Him and tell Him that you do. Let Him lead the decision-making part of your life. This is a sample prayer:

Jesus, I am sorry I have chosen to live apart from You. I want You in my life. I accept the payment of love You gave for me by Your death on the cross. Thank You for being my best friend and my God.

If you have ever prayed a prayer similar to that one, you made the best decision a person could ever make. All other decisions become easier because of the wisdom you gain with a relationship with Christ. It is no longer just you, your wisdom, your strength, your ability, but the moment you receive Christ, God's Spirit indwells your soul and you gain the ability to tap into God's wisdom too. You are now chosen, royal, and part of a holy nation. And as a member of the chosen, royal, and holy family, your message is the message of the King. That is why you are a letter. You bear the seal of the King. In Bible times, when an edict went out from the king, wax was melted and the king set his seal in it, declaring the message had come from him. That is the picture here. Because you have responded to God's declaration, you bear the mark of the King. Everyone who sees you will know you came from His court. You carry His message. This message carries His love, hope, and plan out to others who may not know it yet.

Sometimes we think that because we are bearing God's message the road should be cleared for us. After all, don't the crowds part in the movies when a messenger shouts out, "I have a message from the king!" The crowd then immediately quiets while the messenger reads the king's salutation, and of course they immediately respond in a positive manner, right? Wrong!

A better picture is trying to walk up a crowded escalator going down. We keep taking steps forward but the whole escalator is carrying us the other way. We talk to the people around us and try to convince them to turn and go up the down escalator with us. At first they think we're crazy, but the more we hang in there and keep taking steps forward, the less crazy it becomes.

That's the picture Jesus gives in the Sermon on the Mount: "Enter through the narrow gate. For wide is the gate and broad is the road that leads to destruction, and many enter through it. But small is the gate and narrow the road that leads to life, and only a few find it" (Matthew 7:13-14).

The whole world is walking toward destruction, but they think it's a party and they don't want to hear any different. In Pass Christian, a small tourist town in Mississippi, Police Chief Jerry Peralta drove up and down the highway, stopping at every door. "Evacuate!" he cried. A hurricane was headed their way. Some listened. Others laughed. At one apartment complex, a large group gathered with kegs of beer for a hurricane party. They'd been through a few hurricanes before and they thought they were kind of fun.

The storm hit at ten that night. A wave three stories high crashed in on the apartment building. The building was torn apart and dead bodies were spread across Pass Christian. The next day, a five-year-old boy was found floating on a mattress—the only survivor of the party.

Convincing people of the truth is an upstream battle, an uphill climb, and an extreme challenge. All we're asking people to do is make a 180-degree turn around in life!

I think sharing the good news of God's love is difficult for two reasons. One, we are asking them to commit to a Person who will turn their world inside out to make it better for them, and change is hard. Two, change in the life of someone we share the gospel with may affect our lifestyle as well. It might involve a big commitment of time or emotional energy. In short, God might change our life in the process of changing theirs. We can become selfish, tentative, or reserved because of our own feelings. Here's an excerpt out of my quiet time journal:

God,

Who needs more faith? I'm only asking Lupe to make a 100 percent, 180-degree radical commitment. She's living with a condom salesman who is addicted to pornography, and he's using her up emotionally. But he pays the bills for her and her three boys (two of which are his). I know intellectually You promise to be a husband to her and a father to her boys. I know You can provide exceedingly abundantly beyond all she could ask or think. But, God, I see a woman with no job skills, no naturally bold nature, no Christian family influence—in fact, just the opposite. Sometimes I feel I'm the only voice of truth in her life at all. Yesterday, she brought me a whole newspaper with New Age articles and products in it. One ad even said You had returned and were residing in some channeler's body! It's just me, asking her to follow You!

She isn't the only one with doubts. I know her life and the lives of those precious children will be so much better with You. I know her eternity would be secure in a relationship with You. But I also know the transition from broken to whole will be painful, time-consuming, and scary for her—and me. I'm fearing more for my lifestyle change than hers! I already feel tapped out. All my days are filled with needy people. My heart is so heavy already. I'm afraid I'm turning indifferent because of my lack of faith. I lack the faith that You will take care of this needy lost lamb. I've stepped into Your shepherd's shoes, and I'm afraid I don't fill them well at all. I need You to shepherd us both!

The word "repent" means to turn around. Go the other way. That is not an easy or popular message at times. As people see us battle against the status quo, they may shake their heads in dismay, they may dismiss us, or they may become irritated because we are trying to go up when everyone else is going down. Some will want to follow us because the message of love, hope, and joy is so compelling. But they may be afraid because it looks so hard—but what they don't know is we aren't fighting our way up a down escalator; rather, there is an up escalator smack in the middle of the down one! God carries us up. It is not our own strength that carries us up and out with the message. God carries us with His strength.

In the example above, I was overwhelmed at the impact sharing Christ with Lupe was having on my own schedule. I did step out and do a Bible study designed for those with questions about God with Lupe. She had more questions still! She was hungry to learn more, hungry to have the kind of relationship Bill and I share, hungry to have her children obey like mine did. She decided to send her son to a Christian school before she had made a commitment to Christ. Her son came to know God first. Then her boyfriend was befriended by a pastor on his sales route. (How a condom salesman got connected to a pastor on a friendship level is something only God can do!) Soon I realized there were more than ten strong, authentic believers in Christ ministering to her and her family. I wasn't alone. God had answered my selfish prayer of fear even before He answered Lupe's prayers to know Him.

Can You Criticize a Queen?

If we fear for our time, we fear more that we will be criticized. If we're so royal, if we're so chosen, then why do we get criticized? If we are an envelope bearing such a great message, how do we handle the criticism that inevitably comes our way?

Here's the good news: Even Jesus, who was perfect, was criticized. So when we get criticized, how do we handle it? Here's the process I go through when I am criticized.

1. Is it valid? The first question I ask myself is, *Do I already know this is true?* There are many times when we know even before criticism hits that it is on its way. We all say stupid things, forget when we should remember, react when we should not have reacted. Sometimes we wish we could just push the rewind button of life!

The most vivid example I have is from the first year my husband was in youth ministry. The women's ministry at our church was hosting a mother-daughter special event where the daughter wore her mother's wedding gown. (Now this was already skating on thin ice as the girls were wearing them because the moms couldn't fit in the gowns anymore.) The "models" were to be served dinner first so they could change for the program. The men and youth boys were serving the dinner. One of the older women of the church caught my husband's arm and asked him, "Bill, if I told you I was one of the models, would you serve me first?"

Bill replied without thinking, "Sure, but you'd have a hard time convincing me you were a model." Then it hit him—stupid, stupid, stupid thing to say! He was brand-new at the church, and he came running over to tell me what had happened and ask my advice. Well, we both concluded we might have to float a résumé if the woman didn't extend her grace—which, to her credit, she did.

2. Consider the source. There are times when criticism is launched at you and it really isn't about you at all. Because we live in a society where so many people are carrying emotional wounds and baggage, at any time we can set off someone else's issues and not even know it. One day I went to the post office box to get the mail for our organization, Masterful Living. As I sorted through it, I found I had two personal letters. I read the first one. It was a thank-you from a woman for speaking at her retreat. The letter said, "What you shared changed my life." Then she went into detail about how it touched her. The second had no return address and was unsigned. It read, "You can't possibly be a good mother because you were away from your children when you spoke at our retreat." There was no way to ask this woman what she meant, and because of the postmark, I could tell she didn't know my children or my husband. I had just somehow stepped on an important issue in her life, but because she didn't value me enough to sign it or place a return address or phone number on it, I couldn't give the letter much weight. That day I placed the two letters at the foot of the cross and in prayer said, *God, if there is anything worthy of praise in these letters, I give the praise to You. If there is any merit to any of the criticism, then let specific examples land in my mind. Otherwise, I am going to take every thought captive and plant this criticism in the trash.*

I have found that if I receive verbal or written criticism, and if it is valid, God has already been bringing it up for discussion in my quiet times. If neither God, nor any member of your family, friendship circle, or coworkers see what the critic sees, chances are it is all about an issue in the critic, not in you.

3. Don't let the squeaky wheel receive all your attention. One day many years ago, I walked into my husband's office and found a four-page letter sitting on his desk—all about me! This person had written four pages about what a bad wife, mother, friend, leader—well, pretty much how awful I was in every area in my life. I just sat in my husband's chair and cried my eyes out. I prayed to the Lord, *All I've ever done is try to help—and this is what I get?* Then I cried on Bill's shoulder. He replied with sympathetic insight. "Pam, don't let this one person distract you from the good you do for the many."

Over the next few weeks, that advice echoed in my heart again and again. Each time I would think about the letter, I wanted to quit the ministry. I wanted to stay in bed, pull up the covers, watch Oprah, and eat chocolate—but I didn't. I kept to my mission of encouraging and equipping women.

In this case, I also knew enough about the person to consider the source. The person's home life growing up was close to hell on earth, so I or many other people could have easily set off some emotional trigger.

4. What's there to gain? In this same case, I asked Bill if I should get together with this person and try to talk it out. "I don't think so, Pam. The letter is just ranting. It isn't asking for any solutions or compromises or changes. This person is just raving mad for some unknown reason. No one else feels this way about you, or we would have heard it. What is there to gain? I think all that would happen is that you'd get verbally accosted for an hour or so. You'd feel even worse, and you'd have less motivation to help others who need you." I couldn't help but think about Jesus' admonition of "Don't throw your pearls before swine" (Matthew 7:6 NASB). In some cases, doing nothing but prayer is the best answer. Some people aren't emotionally safe. Even if you tried to iron out the issue, they would attack you. In these cases, step back, separate, and give God space to work.

However, in other cases when I have asked, "What is there to gain?" I have decided that a work relationship would be strengthened or a friendship deepened if I took the time to listen to a critic and follow up face-to-face. I especially find this true if the criticism is a small correction or if it is a correction that is repeated from several people who have displayed loyalty to me in the past. In most cases, I simply thank the people for their concerns, and then I take them straight to Jesus to sort through. By using the process of taking criticism to Jesus, I have much to gain: intimacy with the Savior, perspective from my Creator, and healing of the emotional wound by the great Physician.

5. Bless 'em. The final thing I do when criticism is lobbed my way protects my heart from hardening. It keeps me from cynicism. And it keeps my joy intact. I bless others. After that four-page letter, I sat and wrote thank-you notes to nearly a hundred people in my church, thanking them for their service, their character, and their love. Another time Bill and I were emotionally blindsided by some criticism that really hurt because the person timed it to deflate us after a very special, tender, and meaningful event in our personal life. I did all the above steps, and I was still hurting emotionally. I decided the best way to recoup my joy was to give, and give sacrificially. I then planned and paid for two weekend getaways for two of our most loyal friends in ministry who have helped us shoulder our load. By blessing others, God blessed me with hope when I was hopeless. The thought of bringing joy to other people's lives helped me focus on their joy rather than my pain.

Jayne grew up in a strong Christian home. She was excited about passing on her legacy of faith to her two sons. As they grew, one embraced the faith and the other rebelled. Her mother's heart was broken when she realized her teenage son had slept with a girl he barely knew and didn't love. A pregnancy resulted from that act. Jayne felt as though her son was critical of all the gifts and sacrifices she and her husband had given him. She felt totally rejected. She struggled with wondering how to relate to this new woman in her son's life, a young woman who had deep emotional scars that had made her bitter, isolated, negative, and manipulative. Jayne even struggled with her feelings toward her unborn grandchild. She was hurt and very angry. She was disappointed and disillusioned in her son and in life. She prayed, asking God to help her sort through her feelings. *Give me a way to express love, God.* She remembered the verse in Romans 12:21, which says, "Do not be overcome by evil, but overcome evil with good."

Jayne, who is not an especially crafty woman, decided to crochet an afghan for the baby. With each stitch she asked God to help her work through her negative feelings until she felt love. She stitched and stitched and prayed and prayed until she felt released from the anger. (She told me, "It ended up being a very big afghan!") She knew she needed to give a gift of sacrificial love, a piece of herself and her heart, or she'd never feel released from the bondage of her son's rejection. The afghan not only wrapped the new grandchild in love, it wrapped Jayne in God's protective care.

Decision Points

To be an "envelope" of hope with a positive message to share, you may need to ask yourself some hard questions to gain clarity or confidence:

- What might be keeping you from being God's envelope? Is it fear of failure? Examine how you have handled failure in the past. Are there any changes that make you more able to hang in there or bounce back after a failure?

- Is it fear of criticism? How have you handled criticism in the past? Are there any changes you might want to make to keep you going as you deliver God's message of hope?

- Is it your friendship circle that is filling your mind with the negative so you can't achieve the positive? Look at whom you spend the most time with. On a scale from one to ten, ten being most positive, give all those you are closest to a rating on their ability to be positive. Do you need to make some new, more positive, friends? Do you need to ask the friends you have to try to be more positive toward you? What can you do to turn up the positive "You can do all things through Christ!" message in your head and heart?

- Are you tuning into the truth? Just as a radio plays a clearer message when it is accurately tuned to the correct station number, so your life is able to play a more positive message when the truth of God's Word is turned up in your life. How can you get the truth to play louder in your head and heart? (Attend church? Join a Bible study? Read the Bible each day? Memorize it? Pray it?) Choose one thing that will help turn up the truth.

Decide to Maximize Me

Discern Your Uniqueness and Make the Most of It

One day a man came home from work to find total mayhem at home. The kids were outside, still in their pajamas, playing in the mud and muck. There were empty food boxes and wrappers all around. As he proceeded into the house, he found an even bigger mess inside—dishes on the counter, dog food spilled on the floor, a broken glass under the table, and a small pile of sand by the back door. The family room was strewn with toys and various items of clothing, and a lamp had been knocked over.

He hurried up the stairs, stepping over more toys, looking for his wife. He was becoming worried that she might be ill or that something had happened to her. He found her in the bedroom, still in bed in her pajamas, reading a book. She looked up at him, smiled, and asked how his day went. He looked at her, bewildered, and asked, "What happened here today?"

She smiled at him again and answered, "You know how everyday you come home from work and ask me what I did today?"

"Yes," he said.

She grinned. "Well, today I didn't do it!"

This is something most women feel at some time or another. Shirts in the laundry do not thank us for scrubbing their backs. The dishes don't praise us for the Jacuzzi we fix for them on a daily basis. The towels and sheets don't salute when we walk by.

I did an estimate to see what the financial worth of a home-maker would be if a family had to pay for the typical services mom renders year after year:

Housekeeping	$13,000 (20 hours a week for 52 weeks)
Nursing	$1,300 (1 hour a week for 52 weeks)
Cook	$21,840 (3 hours a day, 7 days a week, for 52 weeks)
Psychologist	$36,400 (1 hour a day, 7 days a week, for 52 weeks)
Taxi	$21,840 (3 hours a day, 7 days a week, for 52 weeks)
Tutor	$3,900 (1 hour a day, 5 days a week, for 52 weeks)
Party Planner	$22,500 (10 times a year spending 10 hours each party)
Sec./Receptionist	$17,472 (3 hours a day, 7 days a week, for 52 weeks)
Total	$138,252

As you can see, most of us can't even afford ourselves! If you add all the hours up, it comes out to about a 35-hour day! We just *feel* as though we have 35-hour days when we serve our family because it is so easy for them—and for us—to forget how valuable we are to them.

Okay, some of us get the perks of peanut-butter kisses from tousled-haired children, or the occasional thank-you grunt of an adolescent who briefly frees herself from the bathroom mirror. There are some of you who get a card, or maybe even a gift, from that wonderful husband who has noticed that only you have radar for whatever he happens to have lost in the house! However, for many of us, it is easy to slide into the "Does anyone appreciate me?" mode after a hard day.

Some of you may also not feel valued at the job that takes you outside of your home. Dilbert cartoons have become bestsellers, in part because they capture the frustration of the daily disrespect many of us experience on the job. In one cartoon, a manager says, "I think you could all take a lesson in corporate respect from What's-his-face here."[1] There are many days we each feel like ol' what's-her-face!

Because we all long for R-E-S-P-E-C-T, we can fall into the false trap of looking in the wrong place for our affirmation. We cannot depend on our husband, children, friends, parents, or boss to give us the validation, affirmation, and reassurance we are looking for. Even if we are surrounded by positive and affirming people, their words will help some, but they will still not fill the void in our hearts. That void can only be filled by hearing from God and believing in His view of us.

You Are More Valuable than Birds

Growing up on a farm in Idaho, there were times that our entire phone and electrical lines were wing to wing with miles and miles of magpies! The sound of those cackling, screeching birds was deafening. At times, a flock chatting to each other would drown out the sound of our television set! Dad would then go outside and shoot a BB gun in the air to send them flying to someone else's backyard.

There are times when we might feel a little like those birds. We chat on about our day, only to have our husband say, "So what's the bottom line here?" or "Get to the point." Or we try to share our thoughts with our children, only to be shut out or worse, "Did you say something, Mom?" We step out in a group to share an idea or opinion, and it is received with a roll of eyes or a "Next!" Some days we feel as though we are being "shooed away" and sent packing. We wonder if anyone values our input or if we really do sound as worthless as a cackling bird.

God cares. He made sure we would know how much He valued us when Jesus declared "Consider the ravens: They do not sow or reap, they have no storeroom or barn; yet God feeds them. And how much more valuable you are than birds!" (Luke 12:24).

Did He say ravens? Are you sure it wasn't only peacocks that He cares for? Or chickens—at least they produce a marketable product. No, it was ravens. Ravens are part of the crow family. They are scavengers, feeding off the dead, and they fly like a buzzard. In other words, ravens are the bottom feeders of the sky. And God still cares for their needs.

But Jesus didn't stop there. He wanted to make sure we got the point. So He looks around him again, and spots an everyday flower. He says, "Consider how the lilies grow. They do not labor or spin. Yet I tell you, not even Solomon in all his splendor was dressed like one of these" (Luke 12:27).

Now these weren't the lilies that we use for special events like weddings and Easter. No, they weren't the gorgeous huge single blossoming flowers of triumph. These were field lilies—much closer in value to our dandelions. They were everywhere. Yet Jesus parallels them to Solomon dressed in all of his kingly splendor.

So how did Solomon dress? No ancient ruler, with perhaps the exception of Alexander the Great, had as much at his fingertips as Solomon. His kingdom was extensive, and monarchs from the entire Eastern world traded with him. The Queen of Sheba visited him, and a pharaoh's daughter was a wife. Solomon had the best fabrics and the newest and most novel bangles, bracelets, and beads available. He had more gold, silver, and jewels than any previous ruler. Those working in his court, including those in charge of his attire, would have been the best available at the time and may have traveled a great distance just to serve this majestic king. It would be like having the entire fashion industry at your beck and call.

What Jesus is saying is that we—normal, everyday, regular us—are as beautiful and valuable to Him as a king in full regalia. We look better to God than a supermodel on a runway in Paris or New York. We are better than a designer label to our Designer.

Yep, you got it. Even in that Kmart blue-light-special flowered housecoat, He says you are valuable. Even on the day you sneak to the grocery store in your painting clothes and baseball cap, He thinks you are special. On bad hair days, good hair days—or no hair days—He thinks you are special.

But because the average person has to hear something at least three times to remember it, God says one more time: "If that is how God clothes the grass of the field, which is here today, and tomorrow is thrown into the fire, how much more will he clothe you, O you of little faith!" (Luke 12:28).

He reminds us that yes, we are finite. Our death will come as sure as the grass in the field. But God cared enough about grass—*grass*—to clothe it in beautiful green. He made that wonderful stuff we love to walk barefoot on. The green carpet we get to mow—and secretly love the smell of its clippings. He says, even though we are finite, and even though we are expendable (there are other blades of grass), He still cares enough to feed us, clothe us, and use us to make the world a better place.

So to sum it all up, from this passage we can surmise that because God cares about bottom-of-the-barrel birds, common-as-they-come flowers, and there's-plenty-more-of-it grass, He will care for us. He will care for us even when we feel so low we could walk under a door, so common we wouldn't even be noticed at a family reunion, or so dispensable we might as well be a paper cup. No matter how we feel about ourselves, God says we're valuable and He will care for our needs personally.

Most of us can handle it if our face doesn't grace the cover of a magazine or our name doesn't make it up in lights. But sometimes, when we don't get the raise we've been banking on, when we come across yet another pile of wet towels and dirty clothes on the bathroom floor, when we come home night after night to an empty apartment, we can start to wonder if anyone even knows we exist.

Some of us are in careers that make us realize we struggle with envy, jealousy, or the "why not me?" syndrome. A professor friend of mine owns a T-shirt that says *Publish or Perish*. Some of us feel invisible to those in charge. The more media driven our world becomes, the more likely it is we will feel sidelined, unimportant, or insignificant. If we don't have a web page, an e-mail address, or a cell phone number, we might not feel in touch, but it only becomes worse when we begin to believe the lie that no one *wants* to be in touch with us. Some days we may feel as though the sum total of our life boils down to a nine-digit ID number.

We don't have to worry about whether others notice us. We are loved by a God who intimately knows us. He wants us to discern the unique gifts He has put in our lives. "We have different gifts, according to the grace given us" (Romans 12:6). A mentor of mine once said, "Guard the gifts God's given you."

The first step to stewarding this treasure is to see yourself and the gifts God has given you as valuable. The second is to decide to discover the gifts and the best ways to maximize what He has deposited in your life.

A New Question

Maybe we are asking the wrong question. Instead of asking if anyone appreciates me, I will get further in life if I ask, "Am I deciding to maximize me? Am I looking for my gift, protecting my gift, using my gift?" Henrietta Mears, the founder of Forest

Home Conference Center and a leader who discipled many future leaders, said, "What you are is God's gift to you. What you become is your gift to God."

I have a set of questions I have used that helped me discover the purpose God has planned for me. Ask yourself these same questions:

What am I good at? List the top ten things you think you do well or enjoy doing. When you are wondering what your passion and calling is, remember that God tends to use us most often in areas He has gifted us in. Because Deborah was a natural leader, God made her a judge. Because Esther was beautiful, God used her beauty to raise her to the platform of a queen who could save a nation. Because Priscilla loved to study and teach Scripture, when a young pastor came through town and his theology was a little incomplete, God used her to equip Apollos, who then went on to achieve a broader ministry himself. Every once in a while, God uses a seeming weakness: Moses confessed to being slow of speech. Well, maybe he felt that way because he'd been out in the desert with sheep for 40 years. He may have felt inadequate as a speaker, but before that he was educated in the palace of Pharaoh. Who better to take God's message to Pharaoh than one who'd been trained right alongside him?

Paul said, "But he said to me, 'My grace is sufficient for you, for my power is made perfect in weakness'...For when I am weak, then I am strong" (2 Corinthians 12:9-10). Paul acknowledged his infirmities, his thorn in the flesh, but he was also keenly aware of his credentials. He lists them in Philippians 3:4-6:

> If anyone else thinks he has reasons to put confidence
> in the flesh, I have more: circumcised on the eighth day, of
> the people of Israel, of the tribe of Benjamin, a Hebrew of

Hebrews; in regard to the law, a Pharisee; as for zeal, perse-
cuting the church; as for legalistic righteousness, faultless.

God took Paul's résumé, changed Paul's attitude, and built a
ministry on the credentials Paul had already achieved. Paul was
both a citizen and a follower of Christ. His Roman citizenship
extended his ministry. His rank among the Jewish leaders gave
him a hearing among a people that were writing off the early
church. It's one thing to ignore a fisherman; it's another to ignore
one of your own. Paul acknowledged what God had built into his
life, and then, because he was humble, God used him.

After my book *Woman of Influence* came out, the first phone
call I received was from a woman in a metropolitan city in the
East who said, "Thank you, Pam! I've been a CPA for years and
never could see how God might use me as an accountant! But since
I've read your book, I have felt compelled to start a battered
women's shelter in our community, and I see how my account-
ing and business background will really help!"

Did God make her good with money for a reason? Definitely!
And will God use the gifts she is good at? Yes! Before a ministry
to battered women can even begin, they need a building, funds,
and ongoing supporters. Will people be more likely to give their
hard-earned money to someone who is certified to take good care
of money? Absolutely! God knows the talents, gifts, and strengths
you have, and He wants to maximize them for His purposes and
plans.

When I had to make a choice on how I would use my college
degree, I saw a variety of options: elementary, secondary, or high
school teacher; college professor; freelance writer; journalist for
a paper or magazine; speaker; director of women at a church or
dean of women; editor; at-home mom; public relations; or adver-
tising. Writing, speaking, and leading came to the surface when

I asked myself, *What three things do I think I do best?* My question then became, "What would make best use of these three things?"

Look at the pie chart (Multiplicity Figure 1) below. Spending your time developing the skills that are most portable will save you time because you are more focused. For example, those students who have a clear direction in college complete their course work in a shorter amount of time than those who keep changing their major. Those same focused students also know what

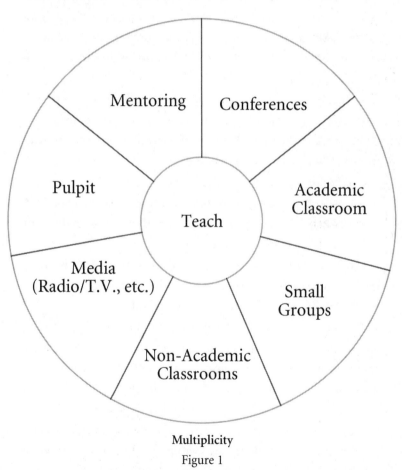

Multiplicity

Figure 1

internships, practical experiences, and training they will need to gain entrance into the job market. Traveling up and down rabbit trails in life will take up valuable time. Focus will *save* you time. In my diagram, the core skills of writing and speaking would be the best portable skills to hone no matter what career change I might have to make.

In an environment of corporate downsizing, constantly shifting markets, and unstable economy, modern women need an abundance of portable skills in order to accomplish their linear goals. Flexibility and adaptability are key components of goals for today and in the future. With persistence, dreams can be achieved by gathering portable skills that will help you anticipate and navigate change.

If this first question is hard for you to answer, ask your friends and family: "What am I good at? What do I seem to enjoy? What do I talk about the most?" Where your mouth is, your heart tends to be too! God says: "Now you are the body of Christ, and each one of you is a part of it" (1 Corinthians 12:27). The context of this verse is that God gives gifts to each member of the body of Christ. You are just as necessary as every other person in the body of Christ because *you are gifted!*

What are you not good at? What don't you enjoy? It is just as important to know what *not* to do as what *to do!* List on a yellow pad a few things in life that you'd rather not do.

I'm not great in the kitchen—Julia Child I am not. I do like to have people in my home, but I have found through experience that I would rather have someone stay for a short while (like a week max!) rather than long term (months or years). Because our world has so many people in it, I find that Bill and I need our home to be a place where there are fewer people expectations.

Does this mean I never cook or have people stay over? No, it just means that as much as possible I try to do what God has equipped me to do. I may not bake cookies for my children's class-room parties—but because I want to be an involved mother, I will write press releases for their school or teach writing workshops. What are the two or three things that stress you out the most?

Saying no isn't always easy. What are some ways to graciously bow out when you feel you aren't called—but you are being recruited?

10 Ways to Graciously Say No to People:

1. That sounds like a wonderful opportunity; I wish I had time. I'm sure someone else will receive the blessing of being involved.

2. Oh, normally I'd love to, but my plate is full. Can you check back with me next time?

3. Wow, that sounds like just the thing _____ might enjoy.

4. I won't be able to, but if you call me in a few days I might have some people I could recommend who would be willing and interested.

5. Let me check my calendar. If you call me in 24 hours, I'll give you a definite answer.

6. You must be so good at what you do! You deserve some people who will be of your same caliber, and I'm afraid I'm not one of them in this area. I would, however, be willing to (make an offer that would fit with your life).

7. Oh, I'm so disappointed! Please place me on the list to contact next time (next year, etc.).

8. No, I can't do that this time. I know I've disappointed you. I know this may even put you in a bind. I'm just going to ask you to give me grace this time. There may be a time I can do the same for you.

9. Please forgive me because I'm going to have to say no.

10. You are such a wonderful person. You know I love you like a (sister, son, daughter, etc.), but I am going to have to say no this time.

What is your time worth? Is working outside the home really helping you financially? Write out how much it costs you to work. Include expenses for items such as child care, clothing, lunches out, an extra car or extra wear and tear on your car, and convenience food or eating out. You may find that you aren't earning as much as you thought. When our three boys were preschoolers, Bill and I did an exercise that indicated the income I would have to earn was larger than his take-home pay—plus I would have missed out on so many intangible and precious moments that the price simply wasn't worth it. Try looking at your talents through different paradigms: working from home, tag-team parenting, part-time employment, and so on. Saying no to a method of working might help you say yes to other priorities.

On the other hand, it might be more advantageous to hire out some tasks to buy more time for the people and activities you love most. Let's say you decide it takes you 15 hours a week to keep your house up the way you want it. If you worked a few extra hours at work, or made one more sale, or budgeted differently, you might be able to hire household help and cut your hours of housekeeping down to three to four per week—gaining a much-needed day off. I find the biggest hurdle some women face is the social or personal pressure they feel thinking they have to do all the housework. Try journaling your spending habits for a month. You might decide to say no to some expenses in order to say yes to some priorities.

Sometimes it's just a temporary no. I try to look at my life through the prism of the seasons. I end one responsibility, for example, chairing the winter retreat, before I take on the role of team mom in the spring. This means I am not a team mom during basketball, but I might be during baseball. Sometimes a yes is even in the no. Because I drive my son to Student Venture each Tuesday, I maximize my time by volunteering to drive his friends, and thus I gain an inside scoop on his life. Because I am there anyway, I often volunteer for smaller servant-type assignments during that hour.

What are my successes? Write five to seven paragraphs on your yellow pad describing times you served others (work, volunteer work, ministry) and you felt it went well (people were helped, encouraged, changed). Why did you enjoy it? Why do you think it went well? (Feel free to go as far back in time as you'd like.) After you have finished, circle or underline any common words or themes.

When I did this activity, I realized that I love to serve best when I am free to be a visionary leader. I love creating something out of nothing. Once things become routine or fall into a rut, I am bored and want a new challenge. So the best use of my leadership and speaking gifts are when I am allowed to have free rein. That's why it suits me to be in charge of an organization—especially one I created to accomplish a predetermined goal. I am more fulfilled in a plan that is flexible enough to allow me new challenges. The church where I serve is a good fit because they are very open to giving me the freedom to run with ideas.

Another pattern I saw when I wrote my paragraphs was the word "teach." It was used over and over, but never in a setting where the schedule is the same day in and day out, or I teach the same material for 25 years! I love to teach when I can also be innovative.

What is my uniqueness? There are some things you do that most people don't do as well as you or with the style and flair you have! Your uniqueness sets you apart. It may be the apple pie you make (and the love that goes into it). It could be your art, your speech, your hospitality, your clear thinking.

Author Daisy Hepburn recommends that you "Do first that which only you can do."[2] I am the only one who can love my husband. (Or else we'll make the tabloid headlines too.) I am the only one who can love my children. Other people can clean my house if necessary—but they can't nurture and train those young hearts. What things do you do that no one else can do?

Leadership expert John Maxwell encourages delegation. If someone else does what you do 80 percent as well, Maxwell encourages delegation at this point. We are then free to do that 20 percent that is unique to us.

When Bill and I were building our home, the project lasted a lot longer than we had anticipated, so our finances were stretched to the limit. For a time I thought we might lose the house we'd worked so hard to build. I remember praying in a quiet time, *God, I'm so frustrated. I can't believe this is happening. We've worked long and hard, especially Bill. I could get really angry at him. He led us into this. But, God, he's the best thing going in my life apart from You. I have had more opportunities to talk about You, Lord, because of the love Bill and I share than anything else. So, God, I'm going to choose, right now. I could nag at Bill, whine, complain, panic, or do a lot of other things—but I won't, even though I feel like it. Even if we lose this house, or if we lose our church because we lost the house, then I'll take that, but I will not let these current setbacks separate me from Bill. I won't let them separate me from You.*

At that moment I *knew* what I had with Bill wasn't just good, it was unique. We had a love that would last. Within a year, we were given our first opportunity to write about relationships—and we still live in the house that Bill built.

One way to make the most of the uniqueness that God has built into your life is the practice of multiplicity (look at Multiplicity Figure 2 on the next page). By taking something that makes you special and using it in as many ways as possible, you save valuable time and you are a better steward of the time and talent God gave you. For example, if I write a magazine article on marital communication, it can also be part of a chapter of a book, trimmed to fit in a newspaper, part of our radio show, or a section of a conference. It could also go on a website or in a video series. One writing assignment has now been used seven different ways and hundreds of more people can be encouraged by the same message sent out in many directions. How can you use your talent in another setting?

My friend Jesse Dillenger is a marriage and family counselor, and she encourages her clients to ask, "What will bring God maximum glory?" You might need to delegate so that your unique

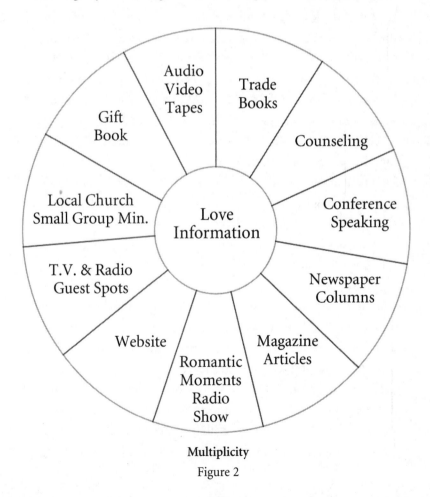

Multiplicity

Figure 2

talents are best used, use multiplicity to expand your time or talents, or simplify part of your life. This way you will have more time in the area you are most effective in touching lives and providing an opportunity for change and growth for God. If we want to be used by Him, we can't be afraid of opportunity just because the people around us may be afraid of change.

What spiritual markers do you remember? Often by looking back we can see how God has uniquely prepared us for our passion. You might have been raised with more than one language or in another culture, or have special training. God is also the master of turning a pain into a platform for ministry. The burning bush was a marker to Moses. He knew God had talked to him at a specific period of time. Moses had other markers too. He was saved when other baby boys were killed by Pharaoh. As he grew, he had to have asked the question, "Why me? Why was I saved?" He was educated in Egypt. When God sent him back to Egypt, who in all of Israel would have been better prepared to speak to the ruler than someone raised in the palace?

You can't do everything—you are only one person. God built your markers into your life for a reason. He uses them to direct your path. Winston Churchill recounted, "I felt as if I were walking with destiny, and that all my past life had been but a preparation for this hour and for this trial."[3]

I have a few markers in my life. My mother put me in a speech contest when I was nine years old. I did a speech on "The Parts of a Lamb," and it won a gold medal. Because my mom and grandmother recognized I had potential, they took me to all the volunteer and philanthropic groups they were a part of, and I either did a speech, a song, a dance, or a gymnastics routine. I became comfortable in front of a crowd. Now while most people would rather do anything other than speak in front of a group, I am at home there. When I reflect on the number of teaching experiences I have had, I know I was meant to impart information. All those experiences in my past are markers to lead me into a focus for my future. Graham Greene said, "There is always one moment in childhood when the door opens and lets the future in."[4]

Markers can also direct you to the people group(s) God wants you to reach. Bill and I met in college at a student leadership conference. Most couples don't marry at 20. And most never get the great training in relational skills Bill and I received. Most aren't given the opportunity to teach and train others in those skills beginning the first day they get home from their honeymoon! Opportunities are a marker.

Luke 12:48 explains the importance of being a steward of the markers in your life: "From everyone who has been given much, much will be demanded; and from the one who has been entrusted with much, much more will be asked."

What legacy do I want to leave? When my grandmother died, all of her grandchildren drove or flew in from all over the country. We hadn't communicated about what each of us would say. But as each one of us came to the podium with what we had prepared, it became obvious what my grandmother's legacy was. All of us, using a variety of words, said the same things about how hospitable she was. She always took time to offer homemade cookies and either milk or coffee to anyone who stopped by. People knew they would always have a place to stay the night—or two—or more if they needed a roof over their heads. She was a great cook and a terrific cheerleader for her grandchildren's dreams. Even though she never completed her own high school education, she encouraged her grandchildren to complete their college degrees and lived to see five diplomas hanging on the wall.

What do you want said about you at your funeral? Each day you are living the legacy you will eventually leave.

What is your mission? If you use the above questions, the answers should help lead you to your mission, your focus in life. Try to summarize what you learned from these questions into a mission statement that explains what you will do, what you want to do, what you commit to do. Here is an example of the mission statement Bill and I decided upon early in our marriage.

We, Bill and Pam Farrel, have a desire to fulfill the great commission through using our skills in professional ministry, with a focus of using the communication gifts God has given us. We are committed to personal discipleship as a lifestyle. We want our home to be an oasis where those who enter can see Christ at work in our marriage and family and where they can find hope. We are committed to fun and friendships. We value people more than things. We prefer memories over material goods. We are committed to raising our children in such a way so they will have the opportunity to experience the benefits of personally knowing Jesus and walking with Him. We are committed to helping them discover their talents and equipping them to help fulfill the great commission and to have fun and a fulfilling life while doing so.

This mission statement serves as a grid. When opportunities cross my desk, I run them through the grid to see if they are worthy of a high place on my priority list. Because of our mission statement, opportunities that allow us to impact others to come to know God personally are highest on the list. Near the top is also memory making for our marriage and family, friendship building, and using our communication gifts.

It isn't always easy to live with the decisions that a mission statement makes clear—but its use is strategic. When the opportunity to write our first book presented itself, we had yet to put a yard in. Our fence was nearly complete but not quite. But because people are more important than things, and because communicating in a way that builds marriages and families is a priority for us, we took a break from finishing the fence and yard. My fence may never impact someone's life for God, but I know the book already has.

Making these choices is not simple, but it is imperative. Dr. Archibald Hart said, "We have to be firm with those who would clutter up our lives with trivia. We must be clear about our own priorities so we can make good decisions about what we will and will not do."[5]

The urgent can become a tyrannical taskmaster. Dr. Hart and a colleague were working on a project with a deadline. It seemed important to them both that the job be done well—but efficiently. Dr. Hart reminded his partner one day, "We need to get it done quickly!" That night Dr. Hart stood over the lifeless body of his friend. His colleague had had a heart attack that afternoon. "Suddenly, my 'We need to get it done quickly!' no longer had meaning. Death has a way of reordering priorities...we move from a worm's-eye view to a bird's-eye view."[6]

A sense of personal mission will squeeze more out of life— and it will help tune your ear to the voice of God. By weighing out the answers to the above questions before God, you are given a framework from Christ. Every decision is then run through the framework, again saving time and energy—energy that might have been spent on worrying before! Focus helps you invest in the life God gave you. Focus helps you spend your time wisely. Lillian Dickson said, "Life is a coin. You can spend it anyway you wish, but you can spend it only once."

When I pace myself and base decisions on my mission, I gain the ability to step back and see the big picture. I can then make choices to find my place in God's plan. When I take the time to see what He has already done in my life, the pieces fall into place more easily. When I look at the pieces God has already laid down in my life, life doesn't look like such a puzzle anymore.

Decision Points

Review the way God sees you in this chapter, and review the mirror. Is that how you see yourself?

Take the time to answer all the questions to discern your gifts and maximize them. What decisions does God want you to make in order to better maximize your unique strengths?

Write a mission statement by using the answers to the above questions. Post the statement somewhere you can see it often so you will naturally reinforce your decision-making grid.

Decide to Be Successful in Each Season

Tackling the Transitions of Life to Get the Most out of Each Stage

Can you believe that average Americans, throughout our lifetimes, spend five years waiting in line, six months at red lights, and one year playing telephone tag? We spend six years eating, one year searching for our belongings, eight months opening junk mail, and four years doing housework![1] (Only four years?) In total, our personal care and travel (mostly back and forth to work) take up half of our lives![2]

Statistics show that women who are employed are working 233 more hours per year than women did 30 years ago. Women do two-thirds of the housework and four-fifths of the childcare.[3] Other surveys, however, dispute the claims of the whining, overworked masses, saying it isn't true they are working more hours. The average person, in fact, is only working a 37-hour workweek.[4] While the average workweek may only be 37 hours, the same time analysts concur that certain groups work more: women in their thirties and forties and those in the baby boom age range.

Half of all Americans say they are feeling more stressed these days, and two-thirds of them say stress affects their health and sense of well-being.[5] In Canada and Great Britain, statistics are similar. In a study of time journals, where people wrote down how they actually spent their time, overall leisure time had been extended—however, it was usually in small increments—so nearly all of it went into watching TV.[6] Television may be the main reason many of us don't feel as though we have more free time than before because we have nothing tangible to show for our time spent watching it.

> Some people are feeling overworked because they have more roles to play…In addition, work may seem longer now because its pace and anxiety level have intensified. The average worker today produces about 30 percent more goods and services than he or she did a generation ago. But the rewards don't seem to have kept pace with the pressures…Complaints about long workweeks are at least correct in the historical sense. Although today's workers may not be putting in the brutal 60-hour-plus workweeks common early in the Industrial Age, they're still working among the longest workweeks in human history. In the medieval era, for example, serfs worked long days in the fields but also had more than 100 holidays a year.[7]

Thanks to laptops, cell phones, Palm Pilots, and wireless modems, you're probably working nearly all the time, part of every day and night. "The dirty little secret of the Information Age," wrote economist Stephen S. Roach in the *New York Times,* "is that an increasingly large slice of work goes on outside the official work hours the government recognizes and employers admit to."

Wireless technology means that tech and knowledge workers can now work all the time—in their cars on the way to and from work, in planes on business trips, in their own homes. We've become tied to our workplaces, and can hardly ever escape. Jon Katz, in his article, "How Many Hours Did You Work," goes on to explain that "odds are shockingly good that you're overworked and underpaid, or, at the very least, not compensated for anywhere near the hours you work."[8]

Time matters. A poem by an anonymous author sums up the value of passing hours, minutes, and moments very succinctly:

Every Moment

To realize the value of ONE YEAR,
Ask a student who has failed his exam.
To realize the value of ONE MONTH,
Ask a mother who has given birth to a premature baby.
To realize the value of ONE WEEK,
Ask the editor of a weekly paper.
To realize the value of ONE HOUR,
Ask lovers who are waiting to meet.
To realize the value of ONE MINUTE,
Ask someone who has missed a train or plane.
To realize the value of ONE SECOND,
Ask a person who has survived an accident.
To realize the value of ONE MILLISECOND,
Ask the person who has won a silver medal in the
   Olympics.

A Clear Focus

Each day provides us with the wealth of 24 hours. How can we squeeze the most out of the time we have in a way that will bring ultimate glory to God, provide for the needs of those we love, and allow us to experience personal fulfillment?

Many of us feel stretched, frantic, and frenzied by the pace of life. How do you know when you're too busy? You're too busy when:

- Cleaning up the dining area means getting the fast-food bags out of the backseat of your car.

- Your reason for not staying in touch with family is that they do not have e-mail addresses.

- You have a to-do list that includes entries for lunch and bathroom breaks, and they are usually the entries that never get crossed off.

- You consider second-day-air delivery painfully slow.

- You refer to your dining room table as the two-drawer lateral filing cabinet.

- Your idea of being organized is multiple-colored Post-it Notes.

- Your grocery list has been on your refrigerator so long some of the products don't even exist any more.

- You are excited when it's Saturday and you can wear sweats to work.

- You find you really need PowerPoint to explain what you do for a living.

- You think that "progressing an action plan" and "calendarizing a project" are acceptable topics for family meals.

- You know the people at the airport hotels better than your next-door neighbors.

- You think a "half day" means leaving at five o'clock.

- You think it's more strategic to buy clean underwear and socks than try to find any in your kids' rooms to wash.[9]

We don't have to feel as though we're trying to hold life together in the midst of a hurricane. There are a few things we can do to gain a sense of surety, confidence, and the peace of standing in a firm place.

God wants us to make the most of our time. He wants us to have a clear focus and a stable life in an unstable world. He even tells us we can do it. Twice He says, *You are standing firm.* Once as a warning: "So, if you think you are standing firm, be careful that you don't fall!" (1 Corinthians 10:12), and once as a compliment, a statement of fact: "For now we really live, since you are standing firm in the Lord" (1 Thessalonians 3:8).

Think about it. Our lives, even as frenzied and frantic as they are, can't be as bad as those living at the time of the first century-church. Because of the persecution of believers, at any moment families could be torn apart, businesses were seized, and people faced being tossed in jail, beaten by an angry crowd, or thrown into an arena to be eaten by lions. It was a war against Christians, who had no place to flee but to God. Yet still God proclaimed to those in Thessalonica, a church founded by Paul's teaching amidst controversy in the busy port city, "you are standing firm."

In the letter to believers in Thessalonica, the apostle Paul commends their focus:

> And we also thank God continually because, when you received the word of God, which you heard from us, you accepted it not as the word of men, but as it actually is, the word of God, which is at work in you who believe (1 Thessalonians 2:13).
>
> But Timothy has just now come to us from you and has brought good news about your faith and love. He has told us that you always have pleasant memories of us and that you long to see us, just as we also long to see you (1 Thessalonians 3:6).

Paul commends how they received the Word and then lived it out. In principle it is simple, but in practicality we have to battle life to stay focused. God tells us that we are children of promise (Galatians 4:28). The context of this section of Scripture is the contrast between Ishmael and Isaac, two sons of Abraham. We are compared to being like Isaac, children of promise. God promised Abraham (see Genesis 15:5) that He would give him descendants as numerous as the stars. God also had a land for Abraham to possess. Key point: Abraham only received the blessing when he camped out on the promise. When Abraham fulfilled his purpose, he enjoyed the promise. When he forgot the promise, and took life into his own hands, then negative results followed. Conflict arose between his wife and the child of the promise and his maid and her child—a child conceived when the promise wasn't believed.

God has promises for us. He promises to give us a hope and a future (Jeremiah 29:11). He promises that truth will set us free (John 8:32). He promises that we will have an abundant life (John 10:10 NASB), a hope that will not disappoint (Romans 5:5), and peace beyond understanding (Philippians 4:7). Key point: When we fulfill God's purpose, we enjoy the blessing of those promises. So how can we sift through all of what life promises to live out the purpose God has for our lives? First we have to figure out why we are so stressed in the first place!

Why Do We Feel So Pressured?

I think the Bible explains the reason why pretty clearly. James, Jesus' own brother, explains the dilemma this way: "Why, you do not even know what will happen tomorrow. What is your life? You are a mist that appears for a little while and then vanishes" (James 4:14).

James is asking the same question we are. What is significant in life? "What is your life?" is a question that could mean "of what character is your life?" James then goes on to give us another of the "You are" statements in the Bible. *You are mist!*

We are all mist and we can't change that. A friend of mine who has had to deal with breast cancer several times has a wonderful answer when people express sadness over her diagnosis. She simply says, "It's okay. We are all terminal." Life is short, and the death rate is still 100 percent.

Not only is life short, God has planned a lot in it already! Life comes prepackaged by Him. Ephesians 2:10 gives us a glimmer of this: "We are God's workmanship, created in Christ Jesus to do good works, which God prepared in advance for us to do." And Ecclesiastes 3:1-8 says:

> There is a time for everything, and a season for every activity under heaven:
> a time to be born and a time to die,
> a time to plant and a time to uproot,
> a time to kill and a time to heal,
> a time to tear down and a time to build,
> a time to weep and a time to laugh,
> a time to mourn and a time to dance,
> a time to scatter stones and a time to gather them,
> a time to embrace and a time to refrain,
> a time to search and a time to give up,
> a time to keep and a time to throw away,
> a time to tear and a time to mend,
> a time to be silent and a time to speak,
> a time to love and a time to hate,
> a time for war and a time for peace.

So there is something to that cynical quip: *Life is short and then you die*. But that sounds a bit harsh and negative to me! I prefer to ask God, "What are the seasons of life and how can I maximize my influence during those seasons?"

A Place to Start

The Trailhead: All of our youth provides the backdrop, the foundation for the decisions we need to make at this important first step of life. When I mentor college students and young married women, I encourage them to use the questions in the "Maximize Me" chapter to make some very important first decisions. What will I major in? Where will I go to college? Where shall I work—for how long? How will I discern Mr. Right? Should I even marry, and if so, when?

In order to unlock her future, a young woman needs to make a few key decisions:

- *Decide God loves you.* The more convinced you are of God's love for you, the more you will listen for His voice and then trust it when He sends direction.

- *Decide you love you.* When you value yourself, you won't be tempted to "settle." You won't settle in your career aspirations; you won't settle in romantic relationships. You won't settle in reaching up and stepping up to achieve in career and ministry.

- *Decide others will value you too.* Now is the time to work through dysfunctional family issues. Don't allow the past to replay in your thought life, and don't allow yourself to become trapped in bad family patterns. If your parents, siblings, and extended family don't treat you with respect, take the high road and treat them with respect. Learn to love unconditionally and learn to set clear, healthy boundaries. Decide you will not be mistreated by family, by friends, by men, or by employers. Don't run away, but you might have to step away long enough to get counseling or input from godly mentors and role models who will help you learn how to balance respect for family with respect for self.

- *Decide you will learn to love.* Learn to take the high road. Learn to be the gracious woman, the woman of integrity, even when it is difficult. I love the necklace Josh McDowell gave his daughter to help her learn how to ask the right questions before she said or did anything. The necklace was three hearts and three question marks reminding her to ask:

Does this show love for God?

Does this show love for others?

Does this show love for self?[10]

The Crossroads: A wedding dress will change a young woman's life. Another person, someone she loves and is intimate with, will change her life—hopefully for the better! But there is another dress that will change her life even more: a maternity dress!

The decision to have children is one that will have long-term implications. Science has shown that children gain more confidence and security later in life if they have bonded to one primary infant caretaker.[11] So the question isn't, "Do I work?" but rather, "How can I become a primary caretaker? How can I ensure a stable beginning and a secure bonding with this child I brought into this world?" When I was pregnant, I was overwhelmed with the amount of information I read encouraging me to nurse because infants get a stronger start physically and emotionally when mom nurses.

Toddlers and preschoolers have a need for a safe environment, freedom to learn, and a small social circle. Selma Frailberg, while a professor at the University of Michigan, discovered that children under three fared best when cared for by mother, and those three to six could sustain absence from mother for half a day, but didn't tolerate well a prolonged absence of ten to twelve hours.[12] The question then becomes, "How can I best see that these needs are met?"

Five Seasons of Womanhood

Finding Focus: Questions for Clarity

1. The Trailhead: Finding my path

- What are my interests?
- What is my major?
- What is my career path?
- Will I have a partner? (marriage/singleness)

2. The Crossroads: Motherhood

- Will I have children?
- When will I have them?
- Who will care for them?
- How much time will I give them?
- How will I make mothering choices (work vs. stay home; education for the child; discipline, etc.)

3. The Evaluation: Midlife

- Who am I really?
- Who and what deserve my time, talent, and treasure?
- How can I find a grid to make decisions?
- Because so much is expected of me, how do I prioritize?
- Are my relationships working? What adaptations do I need to make?

4. The Pinnacle: Menopause and life in the press
  - Am I taking care of me so I can take care of all the people and priorities I love?
  - What resources are available to me for potential crisis (cancer, teen issues, husband's midlife, caring for parents, etc.)
  - Do I have the tools to cope for the long haul if issues arise?
  - Do I have the tools to cope with and protect successes in marriage, ministry, family, and career?

5. The Legacy: Making the most of the rest
  - Am I prepared for the empty nest?
  - What can I do to deepen relationships with spouse, children, friends?
  - What is my mission? How can I leave a lasting legacy?
  - Am I prepared for the final step (insurance, retirement, caring for spouse in illness, my own illness and death)?
  - What must I accomplish before I die?

In my book *The Treasure Inside Your Child* (Harvest House), I talk about the trials and the tools needed to discover the treasure inside every child. This takes time—but it pays great dividends. For example, I went from praying for my toddler, Brock, that he'd quit whining and get a spine to filming his acceptance speech years later when he was named San Diego Citizen of the Year, named Knight of the Year for leadership by the faculty, and when he was awarded scholarships like the one from the National Football Hall of Fame for Scholar, Leader, Athlete. I have had the privilege of buying pizzas for team outreach parties he has hosted, like the one his freshman year where 45 players came and 26 received Christ. I taught him how to start a Bible study for those athletes and that turned into helping him found a Fellowship of Christian Athletes Club on his campus. It all took time—but it was time very well spent!

I know I have a lot of energy and I am a pretty intense person. If I didn't have outside interests all through my marital life and motherhood, I could have been tempted to pour all that energy and intensity into my marriage, my home, and my children. That is not necessarily a bad thing, but it can easily turn into living life through your children or allowing your identity to be based on their achievements instead of your own. Bill has told friends (and our audiences at family conferences) that he is glad I had writing as a gift, as an outlet for my energies, because he and the boys have enough expectations from me already!

So there are some decisions we must make at this important crossroads of life:

🧩 *Decide I will ask God to define me as a wife.* No one knows me as well as God does—even my husband doesn't know me as well. If I look to friends and try to keep up with the Joneses, I will run myself ragged trying to keep up or I will be tempted to pride if I happen to be ahead in the race.

❈ *Decide I will ask God to define me as a mother.* Society fluctuates between placing mothers on a pedestal and giving them total disregard and disrespect. I remember my years as a mother at home. When someone would ask at a dinner party, "What do you do?" I was tempted to pull out my ideological high horse and say something like, "I am a professional who is raising the next generation of leaders." And I have been on the other end of the debate as I have seen women look down their nose at me because I travel and try to mother well and I don't make homemade bread, raise my own garden, or homeschool.

Titus 2:3-5 is a set of verses frequently quoted as we try to make sense of our roles: "Likewise, teach the older women to be reverent in the way they live, not to be slanderers or addicted to much wine, but to teach what is good. Then they can train the younger women to love their husbands and children, to be self-controlled and pure, to be *busy at home,* to be kind, and to be subject to their husbands, so that no one will malign the word of God" (emphasis mine). While dissecting this verse piece by piece, I came across a commentary that suggested that "busy at home" was the woman being responsible for her home, marriage, and children—not that she had to do all the work; she just had to care that the best be done for her family. Our feet can be gone from the home as long as our hearts are still there! Decide how you will keep your heart turned toward home.

❈ *Decide I will ask God to define me as a contributor to society.* Every woman is a unique person. Some women can carry more responsibility than others, but that doesn't mean she is worth more to God. "For everyone to whom much is given, from him much will be required" (Luke 12:48 NKJV).

We are held accountable for our talents and their use. If we are slightly more capable than our sister and yet skating by and not developing our potential, that isn't pleasing God. In the same way, if others have more energy, more intellect, or more time, that doesn't mean we are less valuable.

Instead of living up to our potential by seeking to please God more than everyone else, what we often do is let other voices lead us instead of God's. And if we let others define us rather than God, we will be tempted to just spin plates to keep everybody happy (an impossibility!). Instead of making everyone happy, by spinning plates we'll just end up with a whole lot of broken dishes.

The Evaluation: This is a developmental stage all women go through. For some it is a process of blooming. For those who are unprepared, it may feel like a personal crisis. This usually happens in a woman's life somewhere between the ages of 28 and 38. This is where she will say, "I love my husband and my children, but is this all there is to life—dishes, laundry, and responsibility?" Or she might say, "I have been focusing on a career and now I hear my biological clock ticking." She is asking the big questions of life: *Why am I here? What is my purpose? What is my passion?*

This is when a woman is at great risk for an affair. Often she is going through this stage while her husband is going through his own "Superman" stage, realizing he needs to step up to the plate and not just have a job, but a career because life is expensive! He may be very focused on work and miss his wife's emotional clues. Some women, reading the busy schedule of their spouse incorrectly, then look for someone else to listen to their heart. Often that someone is a man from work, church, the neighborhood— or a computer chat room. She never intended to get into an affair, but as she shifted her emotional needs from her husband to her new friend, the affair happened. (And if you think your life is hectic and complicated now—you don't want to see what happens if an affair hits the picture!)

Decisions that will safeguard your future as you evaluate your life are:

- *Decide you will communicate with your spouse.* He may be very busy trying to build his career and be a good provider for the family, but grab him by the lapels as he runs by and say, "I love us too much to let life pull us apart. Can I have some time with you each week?"

- *Decide you will take your questions to safe circles.* Find a mentor, join a Bible study, pay for counseling, but set up boundaries around your marriage and promise yourself you will not share your time or your heart with another male other than your spouse.

- *Decide to develop yourself.* Don't become a martyr and whine that you never have time for yourself. Instead, look for ways to nuture your interests, talents, and gifts in increments that also fit with the rest of your priorities. Many women bail on their family in an all or nothing mentality mode. Rather, while your kids are in school, finish your education. While your husband relaxes with the guys on the softball field, go to an exercise or art class.

- *Decide to keep your eyes off yourself.* This is the stage of life that women can get ingrown eyeballs. I have heard some pretty outrageous statements from midlife women. For example, "Can you believe it? My husband works all the time. He never has time for me and the kids." (Only to find out that she has redecorated the house, charged up the credit cards, and volunteered her husband for every committee under the sun—and now she is angry at him for trying to salvage their credit rating!) Be reasonable. The world can't come to a screeching halt just because you are in this transition. Your family will still have needs, your spouse will still have a job, your church and community will still value your involvement. I have found that as you stay plugged into real life, God will use real life to answer some of the questions of your heart.

The Pinnacle: You will discover who you are, and you will become very successful at it too! Then your life will hit warp speed. All your children will get schedules, you and your husband may have full, successful careers, and then because of that people will come to you and want your time, your talent, your donations, your wisdom, your resources, and your counsel. It is easy to have some very natural but very tough life stages too. At midlife you could have teens and their raging hormones or be planning and paying for one wedding after another—plus college costs. At this same time, your husband might be in midlife and dealing with his own issues while you are caring for aging parents as you go through menopause! No wonder this is the toughest time on a marriage.

Your husband may be at a place of a reevalution of his own. He is realizing his mortality. He may have health issues that make him long to be young again. When this hits, he can long for toys like a new fast car, a motorcycle, or a new hobby—say, bungee jumping! He may also be wondering if he invested his time well or correctly. He might want to change careers. Some of his behavior might seem bizarre. He may be unbuttoning his shirt, trying to look young, and you want to scream, "Button that thing up!" What he needs at this time of life is not a mother but a girlfriend. So factor in time to date your spouse.

Now you have a recipe for stress because of the insanely full schedule! At this same time, menopause can cause weight gain or mental-pause (forgetfulness) as well as night sweats, hot flashes, or even more serious health concerns. So along with the stress of scheduling, you have some self-image stress as well.

What do you need to decide in order to not just survive but thrive midlife?

- *Decide you will win!* Keep a positive attitude. I started a support group affectionately called "Seasoned Sisters" when my oldest went off to college. At our monthly meetings, we discuss topics relevant to midlife, share resources, pray— and we must bring something humorous! You won't be able to accomplish everything because of a positive attitude but you will be able to accomplish more than you could with a negative one!

- *Decide you will grow.* As the kids leave home, take some of those classes you've wanted to take, take up some new hobbies, develop new friendships, especially ones with women who are committed to have deep and real relationships with Christ.

- *Decide to invest in relationships.* As the children leave for college, as they date and marry and then have children, you will want to have time with family and with grandchildren. This may mean you need to learn new relationship skills in order to relate to and reach out to in-laws. A strong relationship with a son- or daughter-in-law will better ensure the opportunity to develop relationships with grandchildren. At the same time, your husband will be asking for more time with you.

The Legacy: This can be the most rewarding and yet the most challenging stage yet. As you launch all your children into adulthood, you will gain more time. That time will be all yours. You are now wise, experienced, and motivated to leave a lasting legacy.

But facing down losses at this stage can be the most taxing thing you will have ever experienced: the death of your parents, a spouse, your friends, and perhaps even a child.

What decisions will equip you to both leave a lasting legacy and live with strength when the world may seem as though it is unraveling all around you?

- *Decide you will invest in the future instead of just living in the past.* This will keep you feeling alive and well.

- *Decide you will choose hope instead of hopelessness.* Giving up on life will bring the grave even closer.

- *Decide you will enjoy your relationship with God instead of blaming Him for life's transitions.* You'll be tempted to blame God for everything that goes wrong, but that will cut you off from the greatest source of strength you have available to help you. By embracing God, and continuing to study, pray, memorize the Word, and serve, you will keep your mind keen and your heart kind. People are drawn to gracious, mature, godly women.

The Source of Strength

The transitions of life can be strenuous. But God in His love holds out solutions for the stress. While I wrote this book, I was also serving as the executrix for my father's estate. I have become all too aware of what it means to be an heir. The part most people look forward to is the inheritance—the money—but what most people don't realize is that with the money comes responsibility. Part of my job was to ensure that all my father's accounts, debts, and taxes were discharged with integrity. It was my job to preserve his good name with his creditors. I also oversaw the disbursement of inheritance monies to each person named in the will. I know with the money that was given to me came an emotional weight of how to spend or save it wisely. This was a onetime gift. My dad wasn't going to come back to earth and live another life and leave me money again. This was a onetime shot, and my family trusted me to be wise.

That seems to be a little of what God is saying when He calls us heirs. "And you are heirs of the prophets and of the covenant God made with your fathers. He said to Abraham, 'Through your offspring all peoples on earth will be blessed'" (Acts 3:25).

What does God give to us? What is the inheritance? God writes:

> I pray also that the eyes of your heart may be enlightened in order that you may know the hope to which he has called you, the riches of his glorious inheritance in the saints, and his incomparably great power for us who believe. That power is like the working of his mighty strength, which he exerted in Christ when he raised him from the dead and seated him at his right hand in the heavenly realms, far above all rule and authority, power and dominion, and every title that can be given, not only in the present age but also in the one to come (Ephesians 1:18-21).

Wow! Did you catch that? "His incomparably great power" is available to us "who believe"—the same power that raised Christ from the dead. Christ, who sits "far above all rule and authority, power and dominion," is available to help us with our life. Christ, who is given "every title that can be given, not only in the present age but also in the one to come," can help you and me when we struggle with any stage of life. God gives us power. That's why it is the "hope" to which we're called. That's why it is a "glorious inheritance." It's glorious because God's power, ability, creativity, and strength are there to help us walk the walk we are called to. God doesn't say, "Good luck! Hope you can pull it off!" No, He enables us to be usable by living the calling through us by His Spirit, and that pulls the pieces together. My life falls into place with more clarity, and less frustration, when I am relying on His power rather than my own.

Your Fair Share

God wants to make sure we know the inheritance was fair. He tells us the spiritual playing field has been made even. "There is neither Jew nor Greek, slave nor free, male nor female, for you are all one in Christ Jesus. If you belong to Christ, then you are Abraham's seed, and heirs according to the promise" (Galatians 3:28-29).

We are all *Abraham's seed. You are one in Christ.* The point is that "in Christ" distinctions do not exist. Christ is so pervasive in His impact on our identity that all the other indications of who we are pale into insignificance. Race, national distinctions, class differences, political alliances, and gender are small considerations compared to the hope and transformation that exist in Christ. Our nationality, gender, and economic position are chosen for us and create division. "Belonging to Christ" is a choice each of us makes and results in adoption and unity. God's promise to give you the strength and power you need for life is guaranteed no matter your age, your gender, or your race.

"You are Abraham's seed" is a reference to the promise made to Abraham regarding Isaac. Isaac was a gift from God based on His promise rather than Abraham's performance. When we give our hearts to Christ, we get in line with the promise of God that is dependent on His faithfulness rather than on our performance. In the stages of life, sometimes we will be at the top of our game, and other times we may feel down in the dumps, but no matter how we feel, God's power is amply available to infuse us with hope and strength.

We have all we need in Him. Looking for success? You already have it. No inheritance can match the one you already have. Looking for identity? Look again at the "You Are" list that comes after chapter 1. That list describes you and me! We just have to walk in it. Looking for emotional connection? Your Creator wants a friendship, a relationship with you. Looking for security? Nothing can take any of this away from us!

> Though the fig tree does not bud, and there are no grapes on the vines, though the olive crop fails and the fields produce no food, though there are no sheep in the pen and no cattle in the stalls, yet I will rejoice in the LORD, I will be joyful in God my Savior. The Sovereign LORD is my strength; he makes my feet like the feet of a deer, he enables me to go on the heights" (Habakkuk 3:17-19).

Do you want to go to the heights God created uniquely for you? He'll take you there despite your circumstances. No matter what happens, the Lord will be our strength. God will love us through anything.

> No, in all these things we are more than conquerors through him who loved us. For I am convinced that neither death nor life, neither angels nor demons, neither the present nor the future, nor any powers, neither height nor depth, nor anything else in all creation, will be able to separate us from the love of God that is in Christ Jesus our Lord (Romans 8:37-39).

However, citizenship of heaven, the greatest privilege and the most challenging calling, is its own promised land. Paul understood this when he wrote: "Consequently, you are no longer foreigners and aliens, but fellow citizens with God's people and members of God's household" (Ephesians 2:19). *You are fellow citizens.* You are members of *God's household.* You are one of God's kids. "Now you, [sisters], like Isaac, are children of promise" (Galatians 4:28). *You are children of promise,* a promise come true!

God promised Isaac to Sarah. He promised Abraham that He would bless the nations through his son. Against all odds, God made the promise—and kept it. In the face of difficulty, God makes promises to us and keeps them. We don't have to be worried that someone will step on our rights—they will. But they can't take away the promises of God because God has control over them. Decide you will stand on the promises of God no matter the season and you will have success! God promises a reward in James 1:12: "Blessed is the [wo]man who perseveres under trial, because when [she] has stood the test, [she] will receive the crown of life that God has promised to those who love him."

My husband often officiates at weddings and he has the ability to get very young children to stand in place for an entire ceremony. People often ask him afterward, "How did you get him (or her) to stand so still?"

"It's pretty simple. I put down two silver dollars and have the child stand on them. Then I say, "If you stand perfectly still, when this is over you can have those dollars you are standing on."

God's promises are a lot like those silver dollars. Stand on them long enough, and you'll see them come true for you!

Decision Points

What stage of life are you in now? Review the questions and the decisions of that stage. What decisions do you still need to make in order to slide safely through?

What stage is coming? Investigate more about that stage so you can prepare for it. Decide to head to the library, the Internet, or a mentor who has been through it.

Read 2 Peter 1:3: "His divine power has given us everything we need for life and godliness through our knowledge of him who called us by his own glory and goodness." How can this section of Scripture help you in any season? Decide how you can apply God's power better in the stage you are currently in.

$\mathcal{D}$ecide to $\mathcal{L}$ive by $\mathcal{L}$ove

Prioritizing People and the Way You Relate to Them

$\mathcal{H}$alf of all children will witness the breakup of their parents' marriage. Of these, half will experience the breakup of their parents' second marriage as well.[1] In the year 2000, unwed mothers giving birth surpassed married women's birthrate. Nearly a third of American children born since 1996 were born out of wedlock. The illegitimate birthrate is now rising one percentage point every year. In the black community, the out-of-wedlock birthrate is now 69 percent.[2] Half of all single mothers live below the poverty level. Girls in single-parent homes and blended families are twice as likely to drop out of school and get pregnant during their teen years.[3] Girls raised in single-parent homes on welfare are five times more likely to give birth out of wedlock when compared to girls from intact non-welfare families. And a boy from a single-parent home in the inner city is twice as likely to engage in crime when compared to a similar boy who is poor but living with a father and a mother.[4] The teen suicide rate has tripled in the past 30 years.[5]

By the end of 2002, according to the World Health Organization (WHO), 19.2 million women were living with HIV/AIDS worldwide.[6] In 1997 alone, 140,000 women were infected with HIV. Every six minutes a woman is raped.[7] Seventy-four percent of rape or sexual assault victims knew their offenders.[8] One in four girls born will be sexually molested—70 percent by their father or the father figure of their life. One third of all children in juvenile detention centers have been sexually molested while growing up. Four million women each year are beaten by the men they live with—the majority being unmarried partners.[9]

The brokenness is overwhelming! With the world in such desperate straits, how can we "slow down"? Some people have opted for a move to rural America—but many relocate only to find that there are needs in those communities too! They begin serving again, cross-county from where they were. To say, "I quit!" and totally walk away isn't really an option because being a hermit isn't healthy. So what is a realistic option?

Salt and Light

> *You are the salt of the earth.* But if the salt loses its saltiness, how can it be made salty again? It is no longer good for anything, except to be thrown out and trampled by men. *You are the light of the world.* A city on a hill cannot be hidden" (Matthew 5:13-14, emphasis added).

What is the responsibility of salt and light? Salt can be used for many things. Salt is a *preservative*. When meat needs to be preserved for a long time, one option is salting it. Salt is also necessary for life preservation—people and many animals need salt to survive. On the farm I grew up on, we had salt blocks placed in important places to make sure the animals received their nutritional supplement. Salt *cleanses*. Saline solution has been used in the medical field for years for a variety of medicinal purposes. Salt is a *seasoning*. Food just tastes better—especially popcorn—when it is sprinkled with salt. Salt is a *safety tool*. When the roads and sidewalks are snowy, salt is sprinkled on them to help melt the snow and give traction to travelers. Salt helps ice melt at a cooler temperature. When you make homemade ice cream, you add salt to the ice and the ice cream freezes faster. Salt is also added to soft-water heaters to help *break down abrasive elements* in the water so our skin will feel softer and our hair will be shinier. Salt is vital!

So what does God mean when He says we are salt? Just being connected to God makes us unique. We live life differently. Our lives and values help society to be preserved. Having the Holy Spirit reside in each one of us gives the world a conscience because we have an active sense of right and wrong. We also have a God-given desire to help preserve the lives of individuals, much like a nutritional supplement preserves the life of its taker. Our presence cleanses the corner of the world we live in, and just being here helps wear down the corrosive evil that would run rampant if we were not here. We are a safety tool, even though the world doesn't usually recognize it. Our presence makes the world a better, safer, more tolerable place.

For example, have you ever thought about what would happen if you took Christ out of Christmas? There would be no gifts given because it was the wise men that brought gifts to the Babe. There would be no carols—they all talk about Jesus. There would be no tree because it was Martin Luther who first started that tradition. There would be no stars, no angels—well, it pretty much becomes empty. So it is when salt is missing. Life just becomes empty.

But let's look at what salt doesn't do. Salt doesn't scream from the shaker, "Hey dummy, use me!" And it doesn't declare its worth, "Hey, did you know you couldn't walk on this sidewalk without me?" It doesn't take responsibility to go where it isn't, "Oh, wow, look there's a cut that needs to be healed. I think I'll hop right over there." No, salt stays where it is put. Salt does its thing in its place. But salt is pretty much at home anywhere it is put and anyway it is used.

Pat Clary, founder of Women's Ministry Institute, was leading a group of about 40 women leaders. To keep the conference running smoothly, she encouraged us to "stay on our side of the street." What she meant was that if we would simply stay in our area of responsibility and defer decisions outside our realm to the right person in charge of that area, life would run smoother. This is a very hard thing for women to do. We like to care about all areas. But we're just salt, sprinkled in the place God has put us—we can't be everywhere at once. Sometimes the stress we feel is because we've picked up someone else's responsibility, someone else's territory.

This was a difficult lesson for me to learn. When my boys were just babies, I had a friend who was married to a verbally abusive man. She lived far away from me. I gave her phone numbers, I gave her Bible study contacts, I sent her resources, and I told her that if things became life threatening, she could always come stay with me until her husband obtained the counseling he needed. But I couldn't live her life. She had to follow up on the church and Bible study contacts. She had to read the resources and live out healthy boundaries and relationship principles. I couldn't rescue her. Only she could hold on to God, and He would have to walk her through. I had to choose to *give her problems to God and not be her god.*

Not Your Problem!

One day I received a call from a prostitute. She hadn't always been a prostitute. Her husband was a successful businessman, and a mutual friend had been talking with him. He was at his wit's end with his drug-abusing, runaway wife. He never really knew where she was, but his friend said he had a friend who might be able to help—me! She happened to call while my son was napping, so I took plenty of time to talk with her. She was frantic. She hadn't eaten in days. She'd sold herself the night before for drugs, and she was feeling edgy again, as if she wanted another high. She was afraid to prostitute herself again because the night before the john had become very physical and had knocked her around. I kept asking her where she was, and all she would say was that she was in an apartment in San Diego. That didn't narrow it down much! She cried, she whined, she made no sense at times. She told me she had no clean clothes, no clean sheets, and no clean towels, and bugs and rats skittered around her bed at night so she was afraid to go to sleep.

Finally I said, "If you will tell me where you are, my husband and I will come and get you and take you to a battered women's shelter where you will be safe. You can get in a drug treatment program. They have clean clothes, sheets, a warm bed, and good food. I will walk you through it. Just tell me where you are." (I also knew her husband would readily take her back and lovingly care for her—but her shame might have prevented her from that offer.)

Her response was, "Can I take my cat?"

I responded, "Honey, your cat can come with us, but it will probably have to stay at my apartment. Most shelters don't allow pets."

"If my cat can't come, then neither will I." And she hung up the phone. A faceless, downtrodden woman somewhere in San Diego called me, and I had no way of finding her. I wasn't a detective or private eye. I didn't have any high-tech resources available to me the way we have today. There was no star 69 and no caller ID. All I could do was pray and trust that when she was ready, she would call again. We can be available, but we can't live people's lives for them. We're responsible *to* people; we're not responsible *for* them. We are salt. We flavor our section of the world, we cleanse our little corner of society, but we can't *make* someone use the saltshaker.

God also says we are the light of the world. A city set on a hill that cannot be hidden.

Light goes *everywhere* except where there are obstacles to its path. Turn on a light in a bedroom, and the whole room is lit, except for under the bed. Light *travels farther* when there are fewer obstacles and when there is a strong light source. The light of the sun travels much farther than the light of a single candle. Light also *warms*. The bigger the light, the warmer its glow. Light *brings life*. No light, no photosynthesis, no plants. No plants—no food chain—no food chain—no life! Laser beams are light—*focused* light—and they are bright for a very great distance. Lasers can also remove obstacles. When God says we are light, He means we are *strong!* We can illumine the world so people can see God better. We bring warmth and a gentle touch to harsh humanity. We can even focus our energy and remove obstacles in our path. And we are His plan for bringing life, His life, to people. I think salt may represent *responsibility* and light the *authority* to carry out the responsibility. Anyone who has been in leadership knows how frustrating it is to be given a job to do and then not given the authority to make decisions to get that job done. Everything stalls and stalemates. God has clearly given us a job to do in bringing hope, healing, and truth, but He's also given us the authority to carry it out. What is our responsibility?

God's Will Made Clearer

There are only a few statements in the New Testament that clearly say, "This is God's will" or "This pleases God." I believe when we are obeying those statements, then all decisions made while obeying them become God's will. There is freedom in obeying the basic responsibilities God has laid out. Ask yourself, *am I:*

> *Saved*—God our Savior...wants all men to be saved and to come to a knowledge of the truth (1 Timothy 2:3-4).

Spirit-filled—Do not get drunk on wine, which leads to debauchery. Instead, be filled with the Spirit (Ephesians 5:18).

Sanctified—Therefore, I urge you, brothers, in view of God's mercy, to offer your bodies as living sacrifices, holy and pleasing to God—this is your spiritual act of worship. Do not conform any longer to the pattern of this world, but be transformed by the renewing of your mind. Then you will be able to test and approve what God's will is—his good, pleasing and perfect will (Romans 12:1-2).

Sexually Pure—It is God's will that you should be sanctified: that you should avoid sexual immorality (1 Thessalonians 4:3).

Saying Thanks—Give thanks in all circumstances, for this is God's will for you in Christ Jesus (1 Thessalonians 5:18).

Suffering for Right—It is better, if it is God's will, to suffer for doing good than for doing evil (1 Peter 3:17). So then, those who suffer according to God's will should commit themselves to their faithful Creator and continue to do good (1 Peter 4:19).

Seeking God—Blessed are they who keep his statutes and seek him with all their heart (Psalm 119:2). I love those who love me, and those who seek me find me (Proverbs 8:17). If...you seek the LORD your God, you will find him if you look for him with all your heart and with all your soul (Deuteronomy 4:29).

When I realized that all I had to do was *decide* to focus on the basics and my life would please God, a new freedom settled into my heart. I could choose what to do, whom to serve, and where to spend my time without spending hours worrying over the question of whether it was God's will or not. I knew if I simply loved

God and sought Him, the rest of the list would come as a natural result, and the fretting over if I was pleasing Him would be reduced to a minimum.

Pleasing People

How about people? Whom do I please, when, and how often? The new questions became, "Whom do I disappoint and how much?" Because I knew I'd disappoint someone, sometime, and more likely I would disappoint a lot of someones, what would I do with all the guilt?

You will find that the more you have to give, the more people will want it from you—and the people who want it will be more and more in number. But God is very clear. You are just one person! You are *a* light. You are *a* granule of salt. You aren't an entire marquee! You aren't an entire salt mine or bag of salt. All who know Jesus are lights (though some are acting more like a Bic lighter and just flicking their flame every now and again). All of us who know Jesus are small grains of salt who work together toward a common goal of preserving the world He has sprinkled us in. The world doesn't rest solely on your shoulders, even if it feels that way at times.

Jesus makes us a promise, one that seems impossible to believe: "Come to Me, all you who labor and are heavy laden, and I will give you rest. Take My yoke...and you will find rest" (Matthew 11:28-29 NKJV). Irresponsibility aside, how can we live a life that is sane and reflects Jesus' call to rest *and* reach the world?

I try to function from a simple, guiding principle. Now, sometimes I have to fight my way back to it through a busy booked schedule, but I try to camp out on this principle when deciding whom to please beside God: *Some people have earned a greater right to my time.* This seems simple enough, but in reality I have found it is a difficulty for many women to discern who has more right to their time. And women are so busy with the immediate needs of today, many can't even see the long-term ramifications of their decisions.

Who Has the Rights?

There are some relationships that are so vital, so important, that God has established their priority in Scripture. Let's look to Genesis for a peek into this principle. There were three primary relationships that God wanted fostered in the Garden. Man's relationship with Him (they walked in the Garden together, Genesis 3:8), the relationship between husband and wife (the two shall become one flesh, Genesis 2:24), and family (be fruitful and multiply, Genesis 1:28). When Eve listened to the serpent, priorities were forever affected. And when Adam then hid with Eve instead of nurturing his relationship with God, all of humankind has since borne the wounds of his decision.

When God created man and woman in the Garden, He instituted the priority of the family. The family is the first institution—before Israel, before the church, before business and commerce, before community there was family. And of all the family relationships, the husband and wife relationship is preeminent.

When you stood before God and your wedding guests and said, "I do," you made a commitment to place your marriage relationship above all other relationships and responsibilities. For me, I have made a conscious choice to work on becoming an independent mate because that is what Bill needs in me as a helpmate. Being married to a man in ministry, I know that his schedule can take dramatic shifts. He can be called in on a suicide attempt, an emergency hospital call, a runaway teen, or a host of other life-and-death situations. I decided early on to try to keep my life and the lives of our kids as normal as possible, even when the unforeseen arose. I made a choice to do fun things with friends or my children when Bill was out of town for six weeks because of youth work the summer I had a newborn. Other summers, I drove to where he was and stayed in a cabin, sometimes with friends, sometimes with just the kids. Some women would have missed out on all that fun because they wouldn't drive alone, they wouldn't drive at night, or they wouldn't drive in the mountains or anywhere they hadn't been before. I look at each new challenge as an adventure. An adventure to be taken as much as possible with a good attitude.

At times I have had to let traditional roles fall by the wayside. For example, when I grew up, my father always packed the car for trips. But in our home, I have found we can get out of town about three hours sooner if I do all that and then simply drive by the office and pick up Bill. Since I value those three hours, I don't mind lugging a few bags to the car!

Ask your mate this question: "What things, actions, or attitudes on my part make you feel loved and cherished?" You might be surprised at the answers.

Are there times in your day when you know that you will have your mate's undivided attention? Bill and I try to debrief and pray each night before bed. Some couples prefer to talk over coffee in the morning or during a walk in the evening. Somehow, someway, you should talk each day.

Are there times in your week when you can spend a few romantic moments together? Bill and I found we function best when we separate business and pleasure. Once a week he and I exercise and then have a business breakfast where we tackle issues like work responsibilities, ministry needs, and family scheduling. One evening a week we set aside for romance. Sometimes we go out, but often we curl up for a good movie, a candlelit dinner for two, a fireside chat, or an evening walk on the beach. The cost of the evening isn't important; being together is.

But choosing to put your mate first isn't always a romantic decision. Your mate might feel most loved and respected when you stay in the family budget, when you keep the house clean, or when you handle the kids' homework. Your mate also might feel he is playing second fiddle to a career or a school project. Most men can adapt for an impending deadline push once in a while, but no one enjoys feeling as though they are in second place all the time.

People go to great lengths to check their cholesterol levels because they know that if the heart is diseased, the body dies. About ten years ago, Bill and I thought we'd use a few minutes of a date to go to a free cholesterol screening. When we drove to the hospital, we saw people standing in line blocks before the hospital, and they were all there for the screening. I sometimes wish there was a simple test people could take to see if their emotional heart for their spouse was diseased. It would be a healthy sign in society if there were lines of people waiting to see the results of a heart check for their love lives.

How can you tell if your heart is drifting? Each of us has some bells and whistles that should alert us that our marriage relationship is headed for trouble. Take the test below to see how your heart is doing:

1. Are you excited when his car pulls in—or out of—the driveway? (A healthy heart says, "*In* the driveway.")

2. Do you think of ways to spend time romantically to gain more sex, or do you spend more time thinking of ways to get out of intimate encounters? (Your sex life can be a barometer of an overall healthy or unhealthy relationship.)

3. Do you enjoy talking with your husband more than your girlfriends? (You need both relationships, but you should still prefer talking with your spouse.)

4. Are you still dreaming of ways to remodel the house, vacations you can take together, and places you'd like to go—someday? Or are your dreams mostly filled with scenes where you are alone or with people other than your mate?

If you answered in the negative on just one of these questions, you probably need a good vacation together. If two—it is time for a marriage conference. Three or four means counseling is in order.

For our fifteenth anniversary, Bill and I went on a dinner cruise around the San Diego Bay. It was so romantic: candles, soft music, lights on the water. Then the couple sitting at the table right next to ours began to talk about the bills, the kids, and the IRS! Soon their conversation turned into a major argument. It was loud and caused others on the ship to become uncomfortable. Finally, the woman, in tears, said, "We can't talk like this. This is our anniversary." So they quit talking for the rest of the night!

Every year in January, the president of the United States gives a State of the Union address, where he reviews goals and plans and prepares the country for the future. Bill and I have found it helpful to have our own "State of Our Union" meeting yearly where we talk over hopes, dreams, goals, and priorities. On these weekends we discuss long-range goals (5–10 years), short-range goals (3–5 years), and immediate yearly goals. One of the questions we ask on these weekends away is: "When I look back 10–20 years from now, will I think _____ was important?"

All this is fine and dandy for married women, but what about singles? If marriage is such a big deal, how do they decide on priority relationships? After surveying my single friends, they seemed to agree on basically one thing: Spend time with those who nurture your primary relationship with God. For some, parents and siblings still held a top priority. For others, time with a few close friends might be what nurtures you. A key question for singles then is: Is my relationship with God stronger or weaker after spending time with this person?

For every woman, I recommend a few key relationships that I believe form a "success-net" in life:

Mentors. Look for women who have done what you hope to do, who have accomplished and traveled were you long to go, and, most importantly, who have developed the character and depth you hope to grow into. Give these women a call and ask for a few minutes with them. The busiest women may not have many to spare, so offer to serve under them as a volunteer or even offer to help one of them achieve her goal. Ask her if you can be a part of her world in a way that benefits her, and you'll find it will soon benefit you too.

Cheerleaders. Do you remember what slogans those pom-pom girls chanted? *You can do it! Go, fight, win! Victory!* We live in such a negative world that one of the best decisions you can make is to hang out with positive people! Being positive is contagious. You will have more hope and more energy, and achieve more goals if you decide that you will fill your life with positive people who believe in you and in the call and vision God has for you, and who will be there to cheer you forward.

Stretcher Bearers. For many years I was the one who ran to help if someone's loved one died or if their child was ill or in crisis. One month kind of summarizes my need: First, Bill began to not feel well, and he was diagnosed with high blood pressure from stress. He also has a family history of stroke. He was in the middle of a career transition when our son, Caleb, then 13, was hit in football and suffered a ruptured spleen. There was internal bleeding, a CAT scan, a blood transfusion, days in ICU, and eight total days in the hospital where I was by his side 24/7. Finally he was well enough to go home and begin recovery, but he would need to be homeschooled for several weeks. On the day he went back to school, I got some rough news about me from my doctor, serious but fixable. The next day I flew to New York. That evening, our middle son, Zach, was hurt in football, and suffered a concussion and separated shoulder. The following day, fearing he had broken his ankle, our oldest son was pulled from his game. Monday, my brother had a heart attack. (Oh, and did I mention the refrigerator, Bill's car, and the dryer all broke during this time?)

The day I stood in the emergency room, I knew just whom to call to pray, whom to call to help with our sons, and even whom to call to wash our clothes! I knew who our stretcher-bearing friends were. Here are ways I discovered them: (1) prayed with them. Many were in my Moms in Touch prayer group; (2) served God with them. Most had been a part of leadership teams and Bible studies I had run; and (3) suffered pain with them. I had been there with them in a tough time, so I knew they could handle my emotions and my need because they had walked the pain before me. The very best way to get stretcher bearers in your life is to be one in someone else's.

Disciples: Your life will feel more vibrant and more vivacious when you pass the baton to the next generation. Time with your own children or time with others' children, with teens or with other women who need to learn more about God, will bring a sense of fulfillment. To know that your life makes a difference, often an eternal, life-changing difference, will make a positive difference in your life as well. Third John 1:4 sums up my sentiments: "I have no greater joy than to hear that my children are walking in truth." Mary Bethune, one of the first women leaders of the Civil Rights Movement under several presidents, founded Bethune-Cookman College because she believed in giving people a leg up in life. Mary said, "Invest in the human soul. Who knows, it might be a diamond in the rough."[10]

How About Those Kids?

In a survey of 1000 Christian women, Miriam Neff and Debra Kingsporn discovered that two-thirds of women work outside the home. Sixty percent do not work year-round at 40 or more hours per week. The average number of hours worked per week by mothers with children under 18 is 35; for single mothers, 36.[11]

According to Neff and Kingsporn, one-third work because they are single women or single mothers; one-third work because their husband is either unemployed, a student, or employed but in a low-paying job. The final third work because they see it as part of their calling.[12]

The issue of the working vs. stay-at-home mother can potentially divide women faster than anything else. However, I think it might be better if we rephrased the question altogether and asked, "What do my children need, and how can I best meet those needs?" Children need different things at different ages and stages. So the question isn't "Should I work or not?" but "How can I best meet the needs of my children?"

Living with toddlers might mean you change your attitude about what constitutes a "clean" house. You might find yourself reprioritizing. I remember our middle child being very inquisitive and wanting everyone to see everything he saw. Often he said, "Mom, come here." My standard reply was, "Just a minute, honey." Once I walked out after a couple "just a minute, honey's" and said, "Whatcha need, Zach?"

"Never mind. The beautiful butterfly flew away. It's too late. It's always too late."

And he was right. I'd been putting him off more and more. Because we were working in youth ministry at the time, I was reminded that there might come a day when he would no longer want me intricately involved in his life. The more I put him off now, the sooner that day would come because children can sense when you are not interested. I made a conscious choice that day that, as much as possible, I'd come when called to share some exciting moment because the moments would be over all too soon.

School-age children need a strong education, so each year Bill and I ask, "What is best for this child—homeschool, private school, or public school?" The answer to this question may change with each child, geographic location, or a variety of other variables; for example, spotting a child's giftedness and providing opportunities for growth in those areas. School-age children need support to grow and develop an identity, so it's important to address the question of "How will we as a family make sure each child feels supported and their talents and giftedness nurtured?"

Teens need time, lots and lots of time, for you to listen to them as they talk out their value system. Most teens also need some space to fine-tune their giftedness and to have opportunities to hear God's calling on their lives for decisions like romance, vocation, and morality. Ask yourself, "How can I be that listening ear, that sounding board, and the source of opportunity to fine-tune their call? Or do I need to cover other family needs so my husband can be more available to the teens?"

Add to these questions the issues of finances. "What does my child truly *need* vs. what is a *want?*" In the 20 years Bill and I have been in ministry, we have seen great kids come from homes where mom is home full-time, where she works from the home, and where she works part-time or full-time away from home. And the opposite is also true. We've seen kids who are a mess launched from all four environments. So whether to work or not work isn't the right question. Again, the question is, *"Is my heart turned toward home?"*

Are you learning about developmental stages and do you know your children well enough to spot changes in stages and changes in character? There is much wisdom in listening to those who have already been there. As a young mother, I was constantly told:

❦ Spend time with your children while they are young and they will want to spend time with you when they get older. They will want to spend time with you even when their peers aren't spending time with family.

❦ They grow up fast. Cherish those early years.

❦ You don't want to miss those first steps and first words.

❦ The preschool years are foundational. One mother told me, "How they act at four is how they will act at 14—only they will be bigger, and you can't carry them to their room anymore!" (And I think she was right. All of mine have passed into their teen years and their basic temperament is similar to their obedience level and temperament at four!)

❦ Pay now or pay later. That was advice I received about early discipline. And I am glad I spent extra time—and I mean *extra,* in correcting attitudes and behaviors in the toddler and preschool years. My teen boys treat me with respect, and they are responsible and helpful when many moms of teens feel abandoned, fearful, and dumped on.

Who First?

Patrick Morley says in *The Man in the Mirror,* "Set your priorities by who will cry at your funeral." This one really helps if you run your own business or work in ministry. Because Bill's job description includes a large number of funerals, I've really noticed who comes: family! They will fly, drive, or walk if necessary to get to the graveside. The next group that will be there are close friends. These people may have started out as clients, parishioners, community friends, or neighbors, but somewhere along the line a loyalty was built, and you can see signs of that loyalty in your life's crisis points. Who calls to check to see if you're emotionally okay? Who comes to your side in a crisis? Who lends a helping hand during rough financial, emotional, or career stages?

Another question I ask is, "Whom have I chosen to commit myself to?" These people also get a higher priority on my time. For example, if I commit to a discipleship or mentoring relationship, those people gain an inside track so they can reach me easier. Colleagues in business and ministry with whom I have formed some kind of an alliance get their calls returned first.

I also ask, "Who has paid the price to have access to me?" My mother gained that right when she walked the floors with me on sleepless nights. My sister did when she befriended me when I didn't have any friends. My brother did when he protected me growing up. My mentors did when they gave me much-needed advice or a foot in the door. Those who have worked tirelessly alongside me in ministry year after year, either with time or money, gain a greater degree of access. And not only access; these are the people who deserve my loyalty, my help, and my friendship.

Yes, we want to help meet needs, but the need is not the call. Just because someone has spent a lifetime making poor choices and living contrary to God's plan doesn't mean you have to run to "fix" their life when they are feeling the stress of those choices. If we rescue too early, those people may never have to depend on God because they have us. They may also never experience the pain of their consequences, so they then make the same bad decisions over and over because they know you'll come running to the rescue.

So the next question I ask myself is, "Are my actions and behaviors toward others maintaining my integrity and character?" I never want to be flippant when people are in need, but I also don't always have to be the one who meets the need. Just because I am busy doesn't mean I want my standards to drop personally or professionally. When I see myself cutting corners, these become yellow caution lights and I reevaluate. When I start not wanting people to stop by because the house is a mess, or when I feel people have received second best, I regroup, reprioritize, and redelegate. It may serve me well to hire help so I can be more focused on what I do well.

I ask, "Am I reflecting the character of God?" Several years ago I was going out of town and someone called wanting information and books on our ministry. I frantically ran around, arranging how to get the bookstore items they wanted, how and when we might speak, and a variety of other things. Later on the plane, I asked myself, "Why did I think that couldn't wait five days?" Now some things can't wait five days, but in this instance, it could have waited two weeks and it wouldn't have changed anything! The verse, "For God is not a God of disorder but of peace" (1 Corinthians 14:33) flipped into my mind. I tried to picture God frantically running around heaven shoving blessings into FedEx boxes, and the picture just didn't fit! So now I ask, "What are the consequences if this isn't done this minute? Today? Tomorrow? This week? This month? This year?" I then prioritize with long-range consequences in mind and not just by adrenaline or the squeaky wheel.

I sometimes ask, "If I don't meet this need, is there a ministry, resource, or institution that is already in place that can meet the need?" Most often the answer is yes. So I try not to reinvent wheels.

"Am I doing now what will buy me time later?" That's the reason I taught the kids to be a part of the team in keeping the house clean. Yes, maybe those preschool and early elementary years were filled with lumpy beds and half-swept floors, but now it warms my heart to see the boys taking charge of chores like laundry, the garage, dishes, and so on. Because all our boys have had chores nearly their entire lives, we all have more time functioning as a team. This meant I had to give up my ownership and that I had to trust my husband and children to accomplish the same task but in their own way.

A couple of years ago, all our boys had something important on the same night. One son had an award's ceremony, another an all-star team meeting, and the third a ball game. They each thought their event should bring mom out—and of course they were in three different places at the exact same time. (This is now a very normal occurrence!) The more children you have, the more this will happen. The more commitments you've made, the more likely your schedule will have double and triple bookings. So what do you do on days when all the options seem like "A" priorities?

Pray. It may sound simplistic, but regarding those difficult scheduling decisions, after I've prayed one option usually rises to the surface or sometimes creative alternatives take place. My biggest questions are usually, "What is the worst thing that will happen if I'm not there?" "What is the worst thing that can happen if I don't get this done?" A child may feel slighted—not a big thing unless the child senses there is a pattern of him or her getting the short end of the scheduling stick. Maybe it is a missed opportunity. Usually it will not be something that happens once in a lifetime— but sometimes it is. There will only be one time a daughter is crowned homecoming queen, one wedding (hopefully!), one graduation from the eighth grade, high school, and college. On those days the decisions seem clear, but they aren't always.

I was at the Chosen Women stadium event for women where Anne Lotz had been scheduled to speak a year or more ahead. That evening she brought her daughter to the podium and introduced her to the nearly 35,000 women gathered. It seems she and her daughter had a scheduling dilemma to solve. Anne was scheduled to speak the same night her daughter was to graduate from Baylor University. As they shared how they had prayed and weighed out the discussion, the entire stadium rose to their feet and gave the daughter a standing ovation. Her graduation would have been memorable—no doubt—but not as memorable as a stadium packed with women standing to their feet spontaneously and giving *her* a standing ovation!

The principle I saw displayed that night was the teamwork principle. On those tough scheduling days, I bring in backup. I ask my husband's opinion or sometimes my children's. If it is a ministry conflict, I'll ask the people involved. By knowing more of what is planned for the event or meeting, you can often gain the necessary information to make a decision. I didn't ask my children for their thoughts when they were very young (the burden was too adult for them), but as they entered their preteen years, I began to pull them in on family scheduling decisions. I check in with the boys often to see how they think their "mom time" is going.

Recently my oldest said, "Mom, don't get me wrong. I'm glad you care and you ask me, but don't get paranoid. I know you have to miss some of my games to keep shoes on these feet and that your money sends me to sports camps. I'm not going to grow up and write a my-mom-was-a-committed-Christian-leader-so-I'm-dysfunctional book. If I turn out dysfunctional, it will be because I chose wrong decisions. Mom, I'm a leader because you showed me how to be bossy and still love people like you do." (I *think* that was a compliment!)

When talking over some life choices with Fern Nichols, the founder of Moms in Touch, she said something to me I'll never forget. "Pam, sometimes it is the right thing but the wrong time." There is so much freedom in that one statement. We often feel moved and want to respond when we hear about social issues we could help with; for example, abortion, child abuse, teen pregnancy, the homeless, and a myriad of other opportunities in our community, country, or the world. It is at those times I reflect on the timing. I ask myself, "Is this the right time or could I do this later in my life?" Planning for that time when the children have left home, I have an A.K. (After Kids) list that has things on it such as: Take up photography, learn to watercolor, use my leadership skills for the pro-life movement, volunteer for political campaign office work, create a women's center to meet needs of women in transition (single mothers, launchers of home businesses, stay-at-home mothers, returning students, women who want off welfare, women getting out of prison, and so on). These are all good things, and in the past I have participated to some degree in many of them, but right now, because of the age of my children, my activity in these areas is very limited.

So What Do I Do with the Guilt?

You know the feeling. It's the pit in your stomach. It's the cloud hanging over your head. The sinking, shrinking, stinking feeling of wanting to run away, avoid, and cocoon so we won't have to face the person who we think is disappointed in us. It is that "waiting for the other shoe to drop" foreboding that resembles the suspenseful music at the crescendo of a thriller movie. You wonder what price you'll have to pay the piper for going against the status quo. You question over and over in your mind if you made the right decision. Your chest tightens, your sleep is fitful, and your head feels as though it's in a vise. You wonder if the gauge on the blood pressure cuff would explode if you saw the doctor.

This is guilt.

How can you tell where the feeling of guilt is coming from? How can you tell if it is conviction from the Holy Spirit, which you do want to listen to, or guilt from Satan, which you don't want to listen to?

Satan will:

Condemn. He will accuse and replay accusations until you feel like a prisoner on death row. The Bible is clear that "there is now no condemnation for those who are in Christ Jesus" (Romans 8:1).

Condemnation is adverse judgment, strong disapproval, or the result of being judged unfit. It is that nagging, gnawing feeling that you don't measure up to some arbitrary standard and you never will. You're stuck in life, flailing in the quicksand of public opinion or at least in the opinion of someone you disappointed.

Confuse. The Bible points out that God is not the God of disorder. When Satan plays with your mind, he doesn't play fair. He will toss out all kinds of half-truths, partial proposals, and a host of conflicting statements. His goal is to distract you and make you so preoccupied that you can't move forward in your calling. He wants you to be self-absorbed, and he'll throw out distortions and misconceptions in rapid-fire motion to keep you caught like a deer in headlights. Satan's accusations will make you paralyzed, immobile, and stunned in self-doubt.

Cause your heart to become calloused. Satan's accusations will make you overreact. You'll hear yourself say things like, "Who cares!" "I give up, anyway!" "Why try?" "Whatever!" Your goal in life will become selfish protectionism. You'll go from healthy boundaries to a walled-in fortress protecting you from all emotions—not just the bad ones, but good ones too. When your defensive walls go up, everyone and everything will be kept at bay—not just the people who make you feel bad, but everyone.

Connive you into overcompensation. Satan will drive you until you take responsibility that isn't yours. He will whisper lies to you until you feel indispensable, irreplaceable, and like a lone ranger. You'll hear yourself saying, "I'm the only one! If I don't do it, no one will!" You'll fall headlong into the martyr role. You will stomp around the house showing everyone you are the one doing all the work. You'll proclaim your martyrdom to anyone who will listen. "I was the only one here last night. I stayed until 4 A.M. All I did was shower and change. I didn't get any sleep."

The Holy Spirit will:

Be consistent. His promptings will always be in line with God's Word. His prompting will also be the same or similar day after day. For example, I remember God wanting to address my short fuse. I would turn on the radio and the preacher would talk about anger. I would pick up magazines and find articles on anger. I even yelled up the stairs to my sons to quit yelling and Caleb, the youngest, said, "Mom, I don't think God likes it when you yell." *Okay, God, I get the message!*

Be positive. The correction and conviction of the Holy Spirit may be strong, but it is always stated in positive terms. God may point out that an action or attitude is wrong, but He won't call you stupid or bombard you with thoughts of how useless and irredeemable you are.

Be forward thinking. The Spirit will most likely point out "why" a decision was wrong or incomplete. God will remind you of long-term consequences, long-range goals, and eternal values. His conviction will force you to think things through and think things out in an orderly fashion, keeping the end result in view. God will take you to the finish line and walk you back through the race so you can run it better.

Be specific. Instead of vague innuendoes, God will tell you exactly what to correct. He won't say, "Wow, you should feel really bad about yesterday." He will say things like, "Just now, the words you used to talk to Bill were really cutting and sarcastic. Do you want to hurt him like that? Look at his face. Put yourself in his place."

There's No Fairy Godmother, Baby!

Cinderella was a beautiful young woman who had the misfortune of having her mother pass away and her father remarry an evil woman. When her father died, her stepmother and stepsisters treated her cruelly—like a lowly servant. Fortunately, one day her fairy godmother flew into Cinderella's life and created a lovely ball gown and provided horses and a carriage out of a set of mice and a pumpkin!

Many women today are living the first part of the Cinderella story. We are carrying burdens and responsibilities that God didn't design for us to carry. In our hearts we cry out, hoping that a fairy godmother will swoop down and rescue us. But God didn't create life to be lived out waiting for someone else to intervene and change our lives. He wants us to take responsibility for our own life changes. God wants us to *decide* and then work the plan.

Freedom from guilt will not come from a fairy godmother or from someone coming in and flippantly saying, "It's okay, forget it." Freedom from guilt will only come as we learn to discern God's voice from Satan's. "Guilt was intended to drive us to the cross where we will experience forgiveness and freedom."[13] As you sort through the expectations that everyone has about you and your life, remember that healthy boundaries will send you back toward God. He will remind you: You are salt—*one* grain. You are light—*a* light! A woman knows her place in His plan when she knows she is talented and capable but limited, and that *only God* is limitless.

Decision Points

At the beginning of the chapter, you learned that you are salt and light. You also saw that the list under "God's Will Made Clearer" is relatively short. What is one principle or phrase you can hold onto to help you make people priority decisions in your life? Now make a list of the people in your life who have earned more right to your time. Brainstorm ways to keep them a higher priority.

What can you decide today to do that will build up your most vital relationships? (God, spouse, children, siblings, and parents?)

Of the relationships in the "success-net," which relationship(s) do you need more of to have all four corners held up?

Talk to a trusted friend and share when you are most vulnerable to guilt sent from Satan. See if you can recognize some of the common lies he uses to make you feel guilty and defeated. Then replace those lies with the truth.

*D*ecide to *T*ake *G*ood *C*are of *M*e

*Care for Yourself so You Can Care
for the Rest of Your Life*

*Y*ou drag yourself in the door. Your arms are loaded with more work than you feel you can possibly ever get done, so you drop the burden of books, papers, briefcase, files, and bags in the middle of the floor. You don't even bother to turn on the light because you don't want to look at the state the house is in. You're not sure if you want to take a long, hot bath or just skip it all together and collapse on your bed fully dressed. You're hungry, but making anything to eat seems like such a bother. Your head is pounding, your heart is racing, and your body aches. You are sick of coffee, sick of people, sick of demands, and sick of life. You want to lock all the doors and unplug all the phones, pagers, faxes, and e-mail, but even that seems like work. You simply lean against the wall and slide down, collapsing in a heap on the floor. Your head buries itself in your knees and you wrap your arms around yourself because you could really use a hug. You want to cry, but you're even too tired to feel. You are sick and tired of being sick and tired.

Stress and Burnout

In his book *Living the Life You Were Meant to Live,* Tom Peterson notes:

> People often come to me complaining of burnout. I point out to them that they may be approaching burnout,

but they have not yet experienced it. The person who truly becomes burned out has undergone an irreversible change...I have often counseled top executives about employees under their supervision, "You allowed this person to reach the point of burnout. You were insensitive to his needs and to where he was at in approaching burnout. Now it is time to deal sensitively with how you are going to reposition that person."

Executives frequently respond, "I'll give him time off—several months, if need be. That should refresh him."

"No," I advise. "The person has burned out. That particular light cannot be lit again. He has no more value to you, or to himself, in that position or in that department. Find a new area for him. Find a replacement for his old position. The person's talents remain, but he has lost all motivation for doing his old job, and he'll never be able to regain it. *Burnout is irreversible.*"[1] (Emphasis mine.)

Dr. Archibald Hart in an interview with Focus on the Family explained the difference between stress and burnout as stress being primarily biological and burnout being more emotional. Dr. Hart sees stress as "running in emergency mode." The body uses too much adrenaline, the cholesterol goes up, blood pressure goes up, the heart pounds, and the hands get cold. And the result is accelerated wear and tear on the body. Depression can result, but it is the result of physical exhaustion.

On the other hand, burnout is an emotional response that produces demoralization often resulting from feeling a lack of affirmation, depleted resources, and no support system to help you cope. There is a lack of vision and an "I don't care" attitude that develops.[2]

Dr. Hart explains that burnout sneaks up on us. "Our bodies can adapt to circumstances that in the long run are hard on us—

such as when we carry too much stress for too long a period of time. After a while we get so used to it, we no longer recognize it for what it really is—distress."³

Dr. Kwang Ja Park, Director of Missionary Mobilization for Overseas Crusades, sees burnout as a preventable problem in a woman's life. "I see so many leaders, even ones in their 20s and 30s, so tired. They cry a lot. And ones in menopause, they are so tired and cry, I never experienced that." Dr. Park's secret was discovered several years into ministry. In Korea she was a part of a seminary class of 300 men and 2 women who headed out to full-time vocational ministry. After she had been serving as a missionary in the jungles of the Amazon for eight years, she came home on a furlough and picked up a book by a leading pastor at that time. "I don't remember the title, or page number, but I remember one sentence, 'You need two separate goals: ministry goals *and* personal goals.'" She put the book down and registered at Fuller Seminary, not because she needed more diplomas but because learning replenished her soul.

"All this go, go, go, go and do, do, do, do. We become no different than those in business just trying to get ahead. But for the Lord's workers, spiritual growth and personal maturity are so important."⁴

At her graduation from Fuller, she was asked to give a message to her classmates. The message was her life. "Do something for yourself, for your growth, and you will never burn out . . . " She had experienced the principle firsthand. As the first Korean woman to hold a full-time church staff position as a Christian education director at Young Nak Presbyterian Church, Dr. Park saw the church grow from 600 to 8000 in 16 years—and the first ten of those she was in seminary. She went on her days off to reenergize her own life. "Those goals revitalized me." For over 58 years, Dr. Park has laid down her life in service for God, and she is still fresh and growing. How about you? Do you have a few things you do for YOU? What replenishes your soul?

Pursuing R and R

The principle of regular rest is built into the Old Testament. God instructed that one day in seven be for rest, a Sabbath. You weren't supposed to work, travel, cook, or have people work for you—you were to rest in God. You were to focus on how good He'd been to you. Each year in Israel there were approximately 70 days of festivals. With the Sabbaths and celebrations, the Israelites received approximately 120 days off a year. Then God set aside one year in seven for the land to rest. There was to be no planting or harvesting—meaning the farmers had the year off too.

Once every 50 years, there was a Year of Jubilee. In this year there was no sowing or harvesting. During this year all were to return to their home property and clan. Indentured servants were freed and debts were forgiven. While life didn't come to a complete standstill in the seventh-year Sabbaths or in the Year of Jubilee, life was dramatically altered. Most people didn't work. Families were reunited. They were years of reflection, regrouping, and transitioning.

God has also built rest into individual lives. In ancient Israel soldiers didn't have to serve in the army the first year after they were married. In these modern days, are you building Sabbath rests, celebration, and jubilee into your own life? Educators receive sabbaticals to study and rest so they have more to give out when they return. Are you any different? Don't you feel that you give and give and give? Everyone needs time to reflect, regroup, and receive from God so they can be reenergized for life.

What revitalizes you? Is there a gift you can give yourself that will build you up as a person? Many women have grand hopes and dreams for ministry. They have ambitious plans for their children and family. But do you have a satisfying plan for you, one that will develop your inner person? Give yourself a gift—or rather, allow God to give you the gift He has that is waiting to replenish you.

The Gift of Emotional Connection

There are certain behaviors that rebuild and replenish us and give us the ability to go on. It seems even the scientific community has discovered the truth that the Bible has long proposed, "...and the greatest of these is love" (1 Corinthians 13:13). A variety of professionals in the fields of psychology, medicine, and psychiatry are writing on the connection between the giving and receiving of love and good health. In a study at Yale University, scientists studied 119 men and 40 women who were undergoing treatment for coronary angiography. Those patients who felt most loved and supported had substantially less blockage.[5]

Over 700 elderly adults were studied for the effects of aging. The researchers concluded that the lack of degeneration had more to do with what the participants *contributed* to their social support network than what they received from it. The more love and support they offered, the more they benefited from it themselves.[6] In a study of nearly 3000 men and women for a duration of nine to twelve years, those who volunteered to help others once a week were two and a half times less likely to die during the course of the study as those who did not volunteer.[7] (So my mom was right. It is what you give, not what you get, that is important!)

Emotional connections early in life seem to affect our health later in life. In a 35-year follow-up study out of Harvard, 91 percent of participants in one study who didn't perceive themselves as having a warm relationship with their mother growing up were diagnosed with serious diseases in midlife. Only 45 percent of those who described their relationship with mom as nurturing became ill. In the same way, 82 percent who ranked their relationship with dad as low in emotional warmth were diagnosed with severe diseases by midlife as compared to 50 percent, who ranked their relationship with their father as warm and close. If the participants rated their relationship with *both* mom and dad as low in warmth, 100 percent had been diagnosed with a disease by midlife.[8] (This kind of makes you want to pick up the phone and reach out and touch someone you love, doesn't it?)

In a study of postsurgical patients, those who lacked regular participation in an organized social group were four times as likely to be dead six months after surgery. Those who had *no* religious affiliation from which they gained comfort and strength were three times as likely to be dead in six months, and those who had *neither* a religious nor a social support network were seven times as likely to be dead within six months.[9] (Now here's some new motivation to get up and out of bed and get to church on Sunday mornings, right?)

In a study of women with breast cancer, one group received the traditional treatment of radiation, chemotherapy, and surgery, and the other received the same treatment plus a 90-minute per week group session with other cancer survivors for one year. As the women were tracked, the weight of the study showed that those who met in that group for the first year following cancer treatment lived twice as long as those who did not! And all of the women who were not a part of the follow-up support group were dead within five years.[10]

One specialist in this area of science concluded that:

> The more friends you have, the healthier you are. However, this effect is due, almost exclusively, to the degree which you have talked with your friends about any traumas that you have suffered. But here's the kicker. If you have

had trauma that you have not talked about with anyone, the number of friends you have is unrelated to your health. (Social support only protects your health if you use it wisely.)[11]

Dr. Dean Ornish, a leader in the field of treatment of heart patients and prevention of heart disease, was himself struggling with some life choices about career opportunities that were presenting themselves. A friend said to him, "If you are swimming in an ocean and someone offers you a big bag of gold—a golden opportunity—if you take that bag and hold on to it, you will drown. Are you going to hold on to something that will keep you from what most nourishes your soul? Either you let go now, or you become a slave to the very thing you created and it tells you how to live."

Reflecting on this conversation, Dr. Ornish writes: "When my self-worth was defined by what I did, then I had to take every important opportunity that came along, even if a relationship suffered. Now I understand that *real power is measured not by how much you have but by how much you can walk away from.*"[12] (Emphasis mine.)

Do you have the ability to walk away? Those who are task-oriented individuals, like me, may struggle with it most. One particularly hectic day, I was at my desk trying to cram as much as possible into my schedule before I had to pick up my son at school at 2:30. I was racing the clock, and as I picked up the phone and dialed, I looked at my watch—2:30. The face of my precious eight-year-old flashed across my mind. At that moment I knew that the tentacles of my to-do list had wrapped its strong claws into my heart, and the only way to deal with it was with some quick machete action. My kids matter more. I hung up the phone, pushed myself away from my desk in my rolling office chair, and said out loud with conviction: *Pam, walk away. Just walk away!*

Hugs matter. That day they mattered even more because the loving arms of my eight-year-old son reminded me of what is important.

That said, I recognize that walking away is not easy. At one point in my career, Bill and I were leading two growing successful organizations. One seemed to be quite manageable, and the other was causing us a lot of work and frustration. In the first organization, everyone was pulling in the same direction; in the other, we were faced with a tough choice: do some firing, some rehiring, and a whole lot of rebuilding, which would raise both our stress levels even higher and rob us from the needed time to care for our health and our family, or we could walk away and let others lead that organization. I remember the day we had to make that hard choice. I was leaving to go overseas to speak to my toughest audience yet: military wives even as the United States was on the brink of war. My husband came home from a leadership meeting, and he looked terrible. He was pale and his blood pressure was soaring. He crashed and went to bed at 6 P.M. and stayed in bed all the next day while I prepared to go overseas for two weeks. I remember thinking, *God, some things have really changed in this organization. The new leadership is taking it in a whole new direction. It seems many new to leadership aren't emotionally or professionally safe for Bill and me. They don't seem to listen to our concerns or the concerns of our closest friends in leadership. We've tried, God. We've tried over and over. We are running into a brick wall. The price is becoming too high. Help!*

I was upset and frightened for Bill and for our family. I wanted to pack Bill up and take him away with me on the plane. He needed a break. We needed a break. Several hundred people would really be upset if we walked away from that organization, but when I thought of the millions who might lose the chance to hear Bill speak or of the drastic loss the kids and I would experience without Bill in our world, the decision became clear: *walk away.*

Meaningful work is important, but emotional connection is more important, and living out your unique call is most important. Walk away to Jesus. He'll give you the wisdom and strength to walk away from what is unhealthy and walk toward changes that are better for you.

The Gift of Contentment

Meyer Friedman, the doctor who pioneered the concept of the Type-A personality, pinpointed some research in the area of Type-A behaviors. It was first thought that just being a Type-A driving, go get 'em personality made you a greater risk for heart disease, but it was found that only those with one particular component or trait were at high risk—hostility! So it's not moving at a quick clip that is the problem as much as your attitude while doing it!

Dr. Archibald Hart agrees:

> Emotional upsets such as fear, anxiety, depression, and anger can be shown to raise both adrenaline and cholesterol levels…As far as personality characteristics are concerned, two "dimensions" have been found to be associated with elevated cholesterol:
>
> *-overactivity* (excessive competition, aggression, and impatience)
>
> *-overcontrol* (exaggerated sense of responsibility, conformism, and low self-esteem)
>
> Both of these personality traits are associated with the Type-A behavior pattern, which is known also to produce higher levels of adrenaline. Another psychological factor

> contributing to the recruitment of cholesterol appears to
> be that of "perceived helplessness"...when a person is
> caught up in a situation about which he or she feels help-
> less and has no control over the outcome, cholesterol as
> well as adrenaline levels increase significantly...There is only
> one way to diet or exercise in a healthy, stress-lowering
> manner, and that is to avoid frustration, overcompetitive-
> ness, and hostility while you're doing it.[13]

In treating heart attack patients, Dr. Friedman saw that the most striking success at preventing a reoccurring heart attack was to place patients in a supportive small group environment. He said, "Perhaps more than any other thing a leader can do for these patients is to provide them with what many did not adequately secure in childhood—unconditional love and affection from a respected parent figure."[14]

Are you emotionally connected? Are you giving your life away to those younger in age or younger in spiritual growth? Are you allowing your schedule to reflect your own need for emotional connection? Where do you receive love?

The Gift of Physical Care

The best gift of encouragement I ever received was from a colleague who helps busy professionals in ministry take care of themselves. Dr. Earl Henslin told me to picture the gift of exercise in a way that I would be motivated to receive it. He then gave me an example of a person who calculated how much productivity was gained by exercising one hour a day. For example, if exercising one hour a day will help you be able to work an extra hour, then you've gained an hour's worth of wages. Or if exercising one hour makes you more creative, then you've gained the positive outcome of the additional creativity. And if exercising an hour every day will help you live longer, then you've gained years of productivity, and those years can be spent however you and God deem worthy.

For me, having a way to measure the worth of an hour of my productivity renewed my motivation. In my family history, heart disease runs rampant. My father had nine siblings—and most of them experienced their first signs of heart problems before the age of 35! One brother died at 36, and several more in their late fifties and early sixties. Nearly all of my uncles and aunts have had heart surgery.

Motivation to live has been a very real motivation for me to exercise at least some every day. I tell myself, "You will die if you do not work out today." I know God made my body to function under certain health principles, and if I follow them, things work better. But in reality, taking the time to take care of me is a challenge. I have found that if I schedule in twice as much exercise and twice as much time with my family than the minimum we need to function well, then if something gets interrupted, I still have the minimum requirement in my schedule. If I just had the minimum, the interruptions would rob the vitals from my schedule. So if something is vital, schedule it twice as often! (For me the vitals are time with my husband, my children, quiet times with God, exercise, and prep time for healthy meals. What are your vital activities?)

I love the test Daniel threw out to the king's chief official. Daniel wanted healthy fruits and vegetables rather than rich food from the king's table, so he asked the official to test his health against those who ate the king's food. After ten days Daniel's and his buddies' "appearance seemed better...than all the youths who had been eating the king's choice food" (Daniel 1:15 NASB).

Test the system. Some people are motivated when they can calculate the monetary value of a workout. For example, if a business owner or a woman working on commission is earning

$50,000 a year, she is averaging about $24 per hour. The benefit of working out is that she is more alert and clear thinking, so she can accomplish an extra hour's worth of work in the same amount of time, and now she's ahead $24 more a day. If a membership to a workout gym is costing her $1 per day, then each workday she will now earn $23 more because of the added time and productivity. If there are 20 working days in the month, she will earn $460 more per month or $5220 more per year.

If she is 35 when she makes this decision, then she'll earn $165,600 more by the age of 65 than a woman who does not work out. If you add in the fact that she will probably live longer, let's say ten years longer than the average woman, she could earn almost $555,200 more in her lifetime if she works during those extra ten years. Add these two numbers together, and she would wind up with added earning potential of $720,800 over her lifetime by paying $9600 for a gym membership. Working out could net her $711,200. The $20 a month health club membership doesn't look as expensive when you look at its potential return.

I know that money should not be our prime motive in life. But I also know that women, by and large, tend to not value themselves or their time. By looking at the long-term consequences of a decision, through a variety of models, you can sometimes gain a clearer picture of the intangible value of a choice.

If you add to this paradigm the next lens of longevity, meaning that you can personally be healthy enough to actively be involved in your grandchildren's lives, or extend your ministry to the next generation, then the positives of disciplining your life to exercise regularly becomes a higher priority.

Dr. Michael Roizen, professor of Medicine and chair of the Department of Anesthesia and Critical Care at the Pritzer School of Medicine at the University of Chicago, wrote a book called *RealAge: Are You as Young as You Could Be?* Dr. Roizen explained the concept of *RealAge* to me:

RealAge is a scientifically valid measure of how fast your body is aging. *RealAge* is different from your calendar age, which is simply the number of birthdays you have had; your *RealAge* tells exactly how fast you are aging. For example, I am 53 calendar years of age, but my *RealAge* is 38. The *RealAge* book tells us 44 steps that have been scientifically proven to retard or reverse aging, and how much each of those steps changes your *RealAge*. I like to think of *RealAge* as a Currency for Health. If I gave you $50, you would know that you could get your hair cut or buy dinner, but you wouldn't have enough money for a house, and you would have too much for a cup of coffee. That is the potential of money; that is, it lets us value our choices and make decisions that are rational for us. *RealAge* is like money in that it values our choices. None of us will do everything, but *RealAge* lets us know what each factor does to our age so we can make choices that are rational for us.

Dr. Roizen thinks even busy women have options. He says, "Everyone has to make their own choices. What is doable for one woman is difficult for another. Finding out your *RealAge* and choosing what you want to do to make your *RealAge* younger takes just 30 to 40 minutes. And it's fun. And you'll learn how you can gain that 30 minutes back many times over by becoming younger. After analyzing the factors, you can choose to do things that appeal to you to make you younger. Virtually every woman can retard her aging. The program will offer each person specific achievable recommendations."[15]

Dana Demetre, a nurse and health care professional who authored *The LifeStyle Dimensions Program,* encourages women to balance their lives physically, mentally, emotionally, and spiritually. She encourages women to take small steps back to health.

Instead of dieting, Demetre encourages women to think active. "We think our sedentary lifestyle is normal because it is all we know. The average American woman only burns between 1500 and 1800 calories each day. However, in the early 1900s, she burned between 2000 and 3000 each day!…People walked everywhere and engaged in physical labor every day…In order to make long-term change and stay lean for life, you must make a lifestyle change that includes increased activity."[16]

One of the changes I have recently made is to make walking dates instead of coffee dates for those women who are wanting appointments for emotional issues or leaders with whom I need to touch base.

Even drinking more water will help most women. We should drink four to eight ounces of water every hour. If you're awake from 7 A.M. until 11 P.M., then that's about 64 to 128 ounces a day or more than two quarts of water a day minimum. Here's the catch—coffee or cola doesn't count. In fact, for every ounce of caffeine you drink, you need to drink an extra ounce of water! Caffeine is a diuretic, which means it depletes your body of much-needed water.[17] Don't be dismayed. "Small steps, taken consistently, add up in a big way over time," says Demetre.[18]

When we show care for ourselves, we reflect the character of God. God cares for us. He says you are *"a temple of the Holy Spirit"* (1 Corinthians 6:19). You are *"God's temple"* (1 Corinthians 3:16). This means our bodies house the Creator who made them. You became His temple the moment you received Christ into your life.

If God sent me an announcement that He was coming to visit my house, I'd mobilize my whole family into action. Closets and drawers would get emptied and organized. We'd dust, mop, scrub, vacuum, and even do the windows and clean out the garage! I'd go into action to get everything ready for His visit; but He isn't visiting—He already lives here. Because He is always around, I forget how important it is to take care of His place—me! God wants me to look at all my habits and health practices in light of His view of me—a temple. A palace that is holy, houses the truth, and proclaims the good news of love, joy, peace, patience, kindness, goodness, faithfulness, gentleness, and self-control (see Galatians 5:22-23).

Because God interconnected our body, our emotions, and our spirit, when one area responds positively to His plan, all the other areas are affected positively too. The psalmist relays this connection in an example from Psalm 30:10-12:

> Hear, O LORD, and be merciful to me; O LORD, be my help. [A cry for emotional help.] You turned my wailing into dancing; [emotional help came, so there is a positive physical response] you removed my sackcloth and clothed me with joy, [a recap of the emotional help that was received] that my heart may sing to you and not be silent. O LORD my God, I will give you thanks forever [positive spiritual result occurred].

Enjoying the gift of physical health can help you spiritually as well.

The Gift of Prayer

A church decided to test the power of prayer. Eighty names were chosen out of the phone book and the church prayed for them for three months. At the same time, 80 more names were chosen from the phone book, but this group received no prayer. At the end of the three months, both groups were phoned by church members. Of the 80 who had received no prayer, only one responded favorably, but out of the group that had been prayed for, 69 invited church members to visit, and 45 even invited the church prayer teams in for coffee, refreshments—and a time of prayer![19]

Medical science has even linked the power of prayer to patient longevity and recovery. Dr. Dale A. Matthews of Georgetown University reviewed 212 studies and found that three-fourths showed a positive correlation between religious commitment and good health. In a San Francisco study, 393 patients were divided into two groups. Half were prayed for and half were not. No one knew which group they were placed in. Those who were prayer recipients had fewer health complications.[20]

If prayer is so good for others and us, then why is it so hard to accomplish? I think it is because we look at prayer as a task rather than as a relationship. Prayer isn't something I do, prayer involves *Someone* I talk to. For me, prayer is best when I am able to be myself while talking to God. A few things have helped me nurture this relationship.

Know whom I'm talking to. The more I have learned about God, His character, and personality, the more I want to talk to Him. I have studied the names of God, the names of Jesus, and the names of the Holy Spirit. I have done studies on the attributes of God, and I have dug into inductive Bible studies to see how God works with and through people. As I experience God, I gain motivation to pray because I realize over and over what an awesome privilege prayer is. I have a growing confidence that talking with Him will make a difference in my life. When I reflect on His sovereignty and omniscience, that He sees everything, knows everything, and has all power to do anything He deems best, my struggles seem safer in His hands. It is when I stop spending time getting to know Him through Bible study that I wane in my motivation to meet Him.

Know it is okay to be real. Great freedom comes in knowing that God knows everything about me and loves me in spite of myself. For nearly 25 years, Bill and I have enjoyed praying while being real and vulnerable before God. When we pray, if our mind wanders, we simply start praying about that area of life. We assume that because our mind went there, it is either an issue we need to address—or one God wants us to examine. For example, I might start out praying for one of my boys, but then my mind jumps to a work deadline. I'll pray through that issue until I feel peace or release from its burden. Then I'll go back to praying for my son. I will even pray through sinful thoughts as they come. If I'm trying to focus on God and His attributes but a scene from television, an obnoxious commercial, or a cruel thought comes into my mind, I'll pray and commit that area to God. I'll confess that it is wrong and then ask God to take my thought captive. If the struggle lingers, I ask Him if this is an issue I need to address by a lifestyle change. It may be the top of an iceberg exposing a deeper issue.

I also allow my emotions to be real. If I feel disappointed with God, I tell Him. I also tell Him the truth about Himself—not because He needs to hear it, but because I do. I might say something like, *God, I am so sick and tired of people flaking out. If You really do control everything and have all power, and I know You do, how come You don't just* make *people follow through? I know You gave us free will, but I also know You work through prayer. So right now I'm going to ask You to cause these people to* want *to do what is right here! God, I also know I have been lazy and stubborn in my life too, so give me Your grace. But also help me maintain Your standard of wanting excellence—especially since I just feel like quitting like the rest have. Maybe deep down, God, I am jealous because it looks like other people have it easier than me. Help me work through this anger because I can't lead people if I'm mad at them, and I can't lead people if I'm mad at You, so show me why I'm so mad. What am I afraid of? Why am I thinking You owe me? You don't owe me anything. You already gave Yourself on the cross. Seems like that should be enough for me! Why am I offtrack here?* As you follow the thought process of this prayer, you can see that the more real I was, the more yielded I became. The focus shifted from others, to God, and then to what I need God to do in me.

"Real" is different for different people: It can mean crying, pacing, shouting, or being so broken you can't even talk. The key is committing your thoughts honestly to a gracious God, because only then are you free to receive from Him. If I am pretending to be someone or something I am not, whom am I kidding? God can see it's an act! I have found that if I tell the truth about myself *and* tell the truth about God, then answers come.

Prayer is a relationship, not a time slot. I try to layer prayer into my life naturally, but I also try to see that it is natural to set aside time to pray. Yes, I do pray without ceasing. For instance, I am praying right now about how to write these words. I try to look for ways to talk to God. If I am alone in my car, I always assume that my first priority is to talk to Him. I pray as I swim, which in California is several times a week. I also find that walking and prayer go well together because no one can interrupt. I have mental reminders to pray: pictures on my desk, artwork on my refrigerator, and notes on my mirror. I also use specific daily tasks as reminders to pray. For example, every time I fold clothes, I pray for my family. I could choose to sit and watch television or listen to a motivational tape at times like these, but I have chosen to use some specific daily tasks as an emotional buzzer to remind me to pray and talk to God.

Each night in bed, Bill and I pray together. I realize not all women have the freedom to pray *with* their spouse, but they may have the opportunity to pray *for* their spouse.

For many women, praying first thing in the morning and talking through their day with God is helpful. Because I'm not a morning person, I wait an hour or so to pray before I start my workday, and I always pray as I work my way through my to-do list and agenda for the day and weigh out priorities.

I used to think if I didn't pray a certain way (on my knees), or for a certain amount of time at a certain time of day, that I wasn't spiritual. I found that those exterior, self-imposed expectations were actually keeping me from being honest with God. I do, however, like a challenge, so I will take on new goals for this part of my relationship with Him, but I refuse to believe that some people are more spiritual than others simply because they prefer different prayer styles. Comparison can be a trap that will keep you from discovering your own relationship with God.

With different ages and stages of life, our relationship with God will change and adapt. When I was a single woman, I found that I loved to go on picnics or walks with God and spend hours journaling my thoughts to Him. As a young mother, those late-night nursing moments with a child on my lap were my favorite. As my children grow, the car has become my solace and sanctuary. An airplane seat becomes a holy place as I'm strapped in for hours. God then has me as His captive audience, so I save big issues and decisions to pray through on those long trips. I have found it isn't the where or how or how long that is as important as the attitude of wanting to talk to God about all of life. It's the desire of anticipating time with God that helps me know my connection is strong. When the desire wanes, then I know it's time for a kick start: a retreat, a personal getaway, a new idea or routine to wake up my quiet time.

I have already mentioned that Bill and I built our own home. My job during much of the project was to hold a level up to see if a wall or board was plumb or level—in the right place. The goal is to have the level display a bubble in the center of the instrument's markings. If it is not level or in the right place, the bubble will slide off to one side or the other. My own personal peace works the same as that bubble. When my prayer life is in the right place, I sense an emotional peace. My personal peace is like that deep

sigh that usually accompanies me as I step into a Jacuzzi. In a similar way, when I am relaxed and refreshed by God's presence in
my life, I sense a deep sigh in my spirit, and an "aaahhhh" of oasis.
That feeling is an indicator that I am closer to the balance God
has for my life.

The Gift of Celebration

Barbara Johnson, the Erma Bombeck of the Christian community, adds humor and celebration into her life by taking a day
off the first day of each month. I also take joke breaks—all day,
nearly every day. A joke or funny story will take priority over
almost anything. I call Bill and leave them on his voice mail. I drop
by his office and slide them under his door if he's in a meeting
or counseling session. He interrupts my writing often with, "So
have you heard the one …" Humorous books and tapes are a part
of our budget! My friends all know this, so I receive funny e-mails
from all over.[21]

"Silliness is very serious stuff," says Dr. Lee Berk of Loma Linda
University Medical Center. Patty Wooten, a nurse and the author
of *Compassionate Laughter: Jest for Your Health,* agrees. While
Wooten visits patients wearing a clown outfit, Berk and his
research partner, Dr. Stanley Tan, have pioneered a new field of
medicine: *psychoneuronimmunology,* or the effects of laughter on
the immune system.

Doctors showed funny videos to patients and then noted a
measurable decrease in stress hormones and an increase in natural painkillers; a rise in "T" cells, which help organize the immune
system's response; a rise in antibody immunoglobulin A, which
fights respiratory infections; more gamma interferon, a hormone
that causes the immune system to turn on; B cells that produce
antibodies that fight harmful microorganisms; and more Com-
plement 3, which help the antibodies pierce infected or dysfunctional cells.[22]

This field of medicine started when Norman Cousins got relief from his degenerative disease when he laughed his way through funny videos. Even our brain benefits. Peter Derks of the College of William and Mary notes, "When we get a joke, there is a change in brain wave activity; we have solved an incongruity."[23] While laughter is no substitute for traditional medicine, it is great to have such a handy resource to harness good health.

I love a bookmark I picked up in an airport: "No sense being a pessimist—It wouldn't work anyway!"

The Gift of Hope

Laughter is good medicine. So is hope. For most of my married life, one or both of us have run our own businesses. Any entrepreneur quickly discovers it is often feast or famine. When the workload is there, it is often there in piles. When we face deadlines like those, we set up "light at the end of the tunnel celebrations." Just thinking that in a week you might be lying on some sandy, sunny beach with a good novel and great company makes the workload seem lighter.

When I work with women going through the trauma of an unwelcome divorce, I encourage them to do something nice for themselves each day. It can be as simple as a bubble bath or reading a women's magazine, but each day, somehow, they are to give themselves permission to have hope. Court dates are to be followed with dinner out with a safe Christian friend or her support group. Weekends without the kids are times for her to allow God to refresh her life. Conferences, reading a book at the beach, a vacation with other solid Christian friends, can all renew hope.

If you are going through a season of darkness because of a wayward child, a long-term illness, caring for a loved one, or another strenuous life transition, place a light at the end of the tunnel. Plan something into your schedule that will allow you to receive from God.

Throw a personal party. What are some things that cost little or nothing that help you celebrate life? Make a list of these. Choose one thing off the list to do this week. As you celebrate, hope will be revitalized. For example, when I travel through Chicago O'Hare airport, I enjoy riding through the indoor canopy of light and music that extends over the moving sidewalk. I may race through other portions of the airport, but I stop and take my time and just enjoy this brief oasis of art. On less professional days, I sneak off to the children's section of a bookstore and read children's books—without my kids! Or I might host my own personal spa day, which includes a bubble bath by candlelight, a facial mask, and lotion from Hawaii (it doesn't cost more, but I do have to order it to have on hand!). Somedays, the celebration is simply a walk at sunset.

Receive the Gift

Dr. Hart wraps up some words of wisdom that can extend many of our lives: "To avoid cardiovascular disease and other stress-related disorders, it is not enough to eat the right foods and keep cholesterol low. This is important, but it is not enough! It is not enough to exercise regularly and even take regular vacations. To protect yourself…you must learn how to switch off your production of adrenaline when it is no longer needed, and stop using it for non-emergency life situations…It means controlling the problem at its source."[24]

Dr. Hart encourages some simple but practical methods for curbing the overuse of adrenaline: sleep eight to ten hours a night and learn to manage your negative, driving emotions (so next time someone says "Chill out!" take them up on their offer and do it). Exercise and a daily time to unwind will help you manage your addiction to adrenaline overload. He also recommends planning recovery time into your schedule after high-adrenaline-use times. (A side note: Studies have shown that you GAIN weight if you SKIP sleep—wow, that's nice. Doctors are saying it's okay to rest!)

When I travel, I do work on the plane on the trip out, but I save a new novel for the way back. By setting up healthy rewards, the work seems less like work. And the reward system did start with God! "Everyone who competes in the games goes into strict training. They do it to get a crown that will not last; but we do it to get a crown that will last forever" (1 Corinthians 9:25). God will reward us for our work, but notice how the verse begins—with strict training. If we don't watch over our lives, no one else will. God wants you to value you. I like Paul's spin on what a "crown" is. "For what is our hope, our joy, or the crown in which we will glory in the presence of our Lord Jesus when he comes? Is it not you?" (1 Thessalonians 2:19). Paul's hope, joy, and crown were relationships. People were the payoff. *You* are someone's crown. Most likely, you are many people's crown.

When I watch how crowns are treated by homecoming queens, Rose Parade princesses, pageant winners, and monarchs, I noticed they are always handled with care. Crowns receive special TLC. Can you grant yourself permission for some tender loving care today?

Decision Points

How are you taking care of your temple? Are you balanced emotionally, physically, mentally, and spiritually?

What lifestyle choices do you think God would like you to make so you can receive the gift of hope again? Do you need more emotional connection, physical activity, nutrition, or rest, or is it contemplation or celebration that would renew your hope?

Is there someone whose impact on you is unhealthy? *Walk away,* put some space in your schedule, and ask God to show you a more healthy way to relate to that person. (It may mean lessening time with them or going together for counseling, etc.) Is it something you are doing that is raising your stress level? What thing(s) do you need to *walk away from* so you can *walk to* God's best plan for you?

Throw yourself a personal party! Give yourself a gift today. Choose one area to begin taking small steps in. Remember, "small steps, taken consistently, add up in a big way over time!"

9

$\mathcal{D}$ecide to $\mathcal{B}$e $\mathcal{D}$aring

Making the Bold Strategic Choices

$\mathcal{T}$ here is a sin, a secret sin, which someone now is keeping. She tells herself, "It's no big deal, it's personal. It hurts no one…" Envy makes way for jealousy, jealousy makes way for flirting, flirting makes way for opportunity, opportunity makes way for temptation, temptation makes way for possibility, possibility makes way for intrigue, intrigue makes way for excitement, excitement makes way for an invitation, invitation makes way for an affair, an affair breaks a marriage vow, a broken marriage vow breaks:

Her husband's heart

Her children's hearts

Her parents' hearts

Her friends' hearts

Her pastor's heart

Her leader's heart

Her Lord's heart

Her witness

Her future

Her children's future

Her finances

Her secret sin ripples.

There was a sin, a secret sin, that someone once was keeping. It became a sin, a public sin, and now everyone is weeping.

Pastor Tony Folio of Sunrise Church in San Diego is known for saying, "Sin takes you further than you wanted to go; keeps you longer than you wanted to stay; and costs you more than you wanted to pay!"

Bill and I estimate that for the one sin of someone committing the act of adultery, *each* of us then must spend *approximately 100 hours of ministry time* helping all those hurt in the wake of it (and that's if the person repents). That includes time helping the adulterer realign his or her life. If he or she doesn't repent, and continues in the sin and on through a divorce, that number quickly doubles to *over 200 hours* of ministry time taken. And it's not just the pastor's time that is affected. *Every person who is a part of the sinning person's life and is a support to his or her life and family spends a similar amount of time and energy. Hundreds of hours are spent trying to overcome the ramifications of one person's wrong choice.* The sexual act took only moments, but the time it takes to repair the damage is several hundred hours, which could have all been better spent. And it is not just the sin of infidelity that causes such dramatic ripples—*all sin does.*

Compare the hours and hours to the *instantaneous moment* it takes to obey. God's Spirit speaks to your heart, "Don't do it. It's sin."

You say, "Okay, Lord. Thanks for your Holy Spirit's leading." That's it! In just seconds, obedience is accomplished. People often ask leaders like me—and like many of you—how we can accomplish so much. I think this is the key: we obey. (And if we are surrounded by those who also obey, our husband, children, co-workers, and so on, our life is further simplified by obedience.) Obedience saves time! Obedience is a Daring Decision. Obedience is strategic for a woman who wants more out of life!

The Fragrance of Obedience

Just as sin leaves a wake of destruction and devastation, obedience leaves a ripple of hope, joy, and peace.

After seminary, Bill and I came back to the same home church that sent us there and served in youth ministry. One of our favorite families was moving to Atlanta. The circumstances around the move were strained. Carol, now a single mom, was leaving our youth staff to finish a degree program and find a fresh start for herself and her three teenage kids.

They were packing up their beautiful colonial home, and I wanted to stop and say goodbye and offer moral support. I had called ahead to ask if I could come by and if Carrie, her junior high daughter, would mind watching my two preschoolers for a few minutes while I chatted with Carol. Carrie said "sure" and I headed over. I walked in and gave Carol a hug, and then she called Carrie downstairs, to which Carrie replied, "On my way. I'll be just a minute."

I held my two-year-old by the hand as we walked toward the kitchen. I spotted a wonderful antique doll, ready to be carefully packed away. I exclaimed, "Oh, Carol. How beautiful! I haven't seen a doll like this since I was a very little girl. My great-grandmother had one, and I remember I used to love to touch her, hold her, and look at her. They just don't make dolls this beautiful anymore."

"Oh, thank you. Yes, you can hardly find china dolls like that anymore. This one is special. At least that's what I was told by my friend who gave it to me. She was a very kind, elderly neighbor whom I used to help with some things she needed done around her home, and when she packed up her things to move in with her family because of her failing health, she wanted me to have it." Carol had been talking to me from the kitchen where she was making tea. I was standing in the dining room, the beautiful china doll in one hand, and my sweet little boy's hand in my other. I gently set the doll back where I had found it.

I walked a few steps forward, and then I heard a loud crash. I looked over. My son had reached up to grab the fragile china doll, and he held it by one leg. Because he was so short, the doll's head had smashed as it hit Carol's hardwood floor.

I cried. Carol cried. That made my son cry. And then Carol just wrapped her arms around me and my little boy, and we all stood in the dining room crying for a moment. I know I said "I'm sorry" a dozen times. I felt horrible. I had come to give comfort, and here Carol was comforting me. So many of her treasured hopes and dreams had recently come crashing down at her feet, and now I had caused one more broken treasure. I knew I couldn't offer to replace it. The doll was irreplaceable. And even if I could find one somewhere in some antique store, I could never have afforded it. We were barely making ends meet as it was. Carol said something just as remarkable as the things she always said, "I have come to see that things, even beautiful precious things, are still just things, Pam. Relationships are my most valued treasures. Now, let's have some tea." It's been close to 20 years since that morning, and I still remember it as though it were yesterday.

Obedience is like that. It leaves a fragrance of life, health, and hope wherever it is found. Obedience is sweet, and its effects are world changing. How can we cultivate it in our lives?

A Heart-to-Heart Connection

In John chapters 14–17, Jesus relays the most vital information His disciples will need to know as the mantle of ministry passes to them. Over and over Christ emphasizes obedience. He does this in a variety of ways, but the message is all the same. He explains, "He who has My commandments and keeps them is the one who loves Me; and he who loves Me shall be loved by My

Father, and I will love him and will disclose myself to him" (John 14:21 NASB). The secret to being a woman God can use is plainly stated. The answer to how to know God's will is listed. *Obey.* Jesus goes on to try to answer the deeper question of our heart, "But how do we know what to obey?"

"If anyone loves Me, he will keep My word; and My Father will love him, and We will come to him and make Our abode with him" (John 14:23 NASB). When we ask, "What is Your will, God?" we are looking for a concrete list of do's and don'ts. We want a typed to-do list. We want the meeting's agenda. But God wants a *connection* with us.

You Are the Branches

In John 15:1-17 Jesus gives us a picture of our relationship with Him. "I am the vine; you are the branches" (John 15:5). This is a picture of the vineyards so common in the hills and valleys of Israel. Jesus is the vine. All the nutrients come from Him. His roots sink into the ground to gather all we need, and then He supplies it all to us. All we have to do is receive it and blossom! We aren't just any kind of branch—we're a pruned branch. "Every branch that does bear fruit he prunes so that it will be even more fruitful. You are already clean because of the word I have spoken to you" (John 15:2-3). *You are clean,* ready to grow, and prepared for fruitfulness.

As clean branches, we cannot decide to just take off and do our own thing. We'd die. A branch must be connected to the vine to produce fruit. That's why Jesus finishes verse 5, "he who abides in Me and I in him, he bears much fruit; for apart from Me you can do nothing" (NASB).

No abiding, no fruit. It is like a math formula: A + B = C. Jesus in me + me abiding in Him = fruit. So what does abiding mean, and how do we do it? In this case the meaning is to *stay,* continue, dwell, endure, be present, remain, stand, tarry—in other words, don't go anywhere![1] It's as though we're pitching a tent and we've taken up residence in Him. I like to say I am camping out in who God is.

The results of abiding are given in verse 11. "These things I have spoken to you so that My joy may be in you, and that your joy may be made full" (NASB). And isn't joy one of the things we women are really after? We love the feeling of being on top of the world, at peace with ourselves and those around us. We love the excitement and adventure of seeing a plan come together. We love the rush, the jazz, the thrill of deep emotional connectedness. Wrap up all those emotions and a few other positive feelings, and that's how we picture joy. Jesus is saying that the deep "everything will work out no matter what" peace is His joy, and it only comes to us when we abide. There is no other way to have the sense that the pieces are falling together. It only comes when we abide, stay, remain, or *camp out* in Him!

You Are Friends

Jesus moves to a new picture, a more intimate one. In verse 15 He says, "No longer do I call you slaves, for the slave does not know what his master is doing; but I have called you friends, for all things that I have heard from My Father I have made known to you" (NASB). Jesus has the right to call us slaves or servants. After all, we were bought with a price—His blood. But He wants us to be more than people who "owe Him." He knows how our minds work.

Have you ever owed someone money? Every time you see them you feel guilty. You know that they know that you owe them. They may not act differently toward you than before, but you know there is something there, and neither of you has to say anything. If you go on owing, you may even want to avoid seeing that person altogether because you feel so bad about not repaying. Jesus doesn't want a strained relationship built on a foundation of guilt. He wants to be our friend, even though we still owe Him and always will! He knows there is no amount of money, there is no amount of good works, there is nothing we can do that will repay what He did for us on Calvary, so He changes the relationship entirely. He calls us friends.

My best friend wants what is best for me. She is willing to be inconvenienced to see that I have what I need to succeed in all of my life, home, work, ministry, and relationships. She and I talk regularly, and when we talk it is on a deeper level. She can tell from my voice over the phone when I'm stressed or discouraged. She can tell from my body language if I am feeling great or anxious.

If I describe my friendship with my husband, I would also add that he wants to know all about me and I want to know all about him. We would go to the ends of the earth to help each other out. I know he would die for me. I know he would set aside his wants, needs, and desires if I needed him to. When we are separated by ministry or business, we feel the strain of being apart. I once told him, "Honey, I'm just no good without you." I feel that when we are together we are so much stronger, we think clearer, and we make a winning team.

Friendship with Jesus is *all* that and so much more. He knows our every thought. He knows our every need even before we do. He sees our lives in totality and how they relate to the framework of history, and He can work all things for our good. He created time, so He can see from beginning to end what is best for us, and He has the power to carry out all the plans He has for us. He placed His Holy Spirit in us, and He describes the fruit the Holy Spirit will produce in our lives if we are yielded: "Love, joy, peace, patience, kindness, goodness, faithfulness, gentleness and self-control" (Galatians 5:22-23). In John 16, He says the Holy Spirit convicts concerning sin, righteousness, and judgment, and He will lead us into all truth, and He will glorify God (see John 16:8,13-14).

If I am a friend of God, I will want to know all about Him. As I know about Him, then I will know what He wants me to do.

The Big Picture

There are certain methods that have helped me know God's will. I like to parallel them to the same way we learn to interpret Scripture. If I am lost in a city, I pick up a map. If I don't have one, I go to the highest point I can find so I can get my bearings by looking at the big picture. The same thing is true of discerning God's will. Women who have taken the time, energy, and work to study the Bible cover to cover are more confident in their own ability to hear God's voice. Having an overall understanding of God's Word helps us understand God and understand how He works. By layering the big picture into your life on a regular basis, your framework for hearing the voice of God stays in place.

Try one of these ideas to layer the big picture into your life:

Read the Bible through in a year. There are many great programs to help you do this. Your own Bible might even have a plan for accomplishing this in a year. The *One Year Bible* (Tyndale) is also a resource you might consider. My favorite way to read the Bible through is a quiet time resource called *Walk Thru the Bible.*[2] It is a magazine that comes monthly to your home, and it daily leads you devotionally through the Bible. It has information on history, charts, diagrams, and practical inspirational thoughts to feed you emotionally, spiritually, and intellectually.

Study the Bible chronologically. I have a poster in my office that explains how the Bible came from its original papyrus form to the Bible in my own language that sits on my desk today. Seeing the Bible and how God has sustained His Word gives me confidence that He will sustain me too. As I see how God has had a plan for men and women throughout history, I am reassured that He has a plan for me too. I also enjoy the *Chronological Bible* (Tyndale), which is compiled in the order the books were written. By seeing the chronology, I get the point driven home devotionally that God is a God of order. He lays foundations and then builds on them. He called Israel and gave her a mission to exhibit His character to all who came in contact with her. He established the family. He called Abraham, and then Moses, to lead a nation, a chosen one. He set down the law so it would be a tutor of right and wrong. The law showed people that, on their own, they couldn't meet the standard. When they needed a Savior, He sent a Savior.

By seeing the big picture, I gain a philosophy of life that is the backdrop to my daily decisions. For example, because God first laid down the law and *then* held men accountable for it, as a parent I should also instruct before I discipline. How can people obey when they didn't know there was a rule to obey? Because God is a God of order, and He has moved patiently throughout history, if I am rushing around forcing a decision, and everything seems unsure, unclear, and confusing, then chances are this decision isn't His will. Because I see over and over again that God came to individual people with a calling, even when He was giving instructions for entire nations, I should assume that God today will call individuals and then build a ministry around them. That God blesses people and not programs is a philosophy I picked up from seeing the big picture.

I might feel overwhelmed if I think I have to single-handedly turn the morality of a nation back to God, but if I go back to the big picture, I will see that God worked with leaders and squared away their integrity, and then there was a trickledown effect that took place among the people. I can watch over my own integrity, and I don't have to think I am a watchdog for the world's. The impossible just became possible because I stepped back and took a look at the big picture.

Get to know the character of God. By doing theme studies of the Bible, as in what the Bible says about money, sex, power, children, and mothering, I gain an overall picture of God's heart on any given subject. It helps me get to know the character of God better. Study His names. The names of the Father, the Son, and the Holy Spirit will all reveal who God is in a rich way. By studying who God is, I get to see how He thinks, acts, and relates to people. When I am in a tough spot, especially when I have to make a quick decision, I go back and ask: "What would God's character have me do?" I find encouragement in1 John 4:16, "God is love. Whoever lives in love lives in God, and God in him." So when I wonder what is strategic, what is the best decision, I ask, "What would love do?"

Look at things in context. A key point in learning to accurately interpret the Bible is to look at a verse within its context. What verses are around it, what chapter comes before and after, and what are those chapters talking about? What book is it in? Who wrote that book, to whom was it written, and why? As I look at the context of a verse, I gain clarity on its meaning.

I have found the same thing to be true in decision making. When people hire employees, they often do background checks and references. That is one way of looking at a person in his or her context. Before I allowed my children to go to a person's home, I accompanied them. By seeing someone's surroundings, you learn a lot about them, their values, and their priorities.

Focusing the Picture

After looking at the big picture, you next start to narrow your field of scope. As you study the Bible, you can make outlines, diagram sentences, and do word studies. When making a decision,

I like to have as much information as possible in front of me. It is not uncommon for me to say, "I will have to get back to you on that. I need more information to make an informed decision." I make charts, pros-and-cons lists, and graphs if I think they will help me see the issue in a clearer light.

When you layer God's Word into your life on a daily basis, you gain the ability to see things closer to the way God does. Jesus explains it as "you are in me and I am in you" (John 14:20). Paul tells us, "We have the mind of Christ" (1 Corinthians 2:16).

The Word of God points out how important it is to protect our hearts. "Above all else, guard your heart, for it is the wellspring of life" (Proverbs 4:23). My son Zach is a skateboarder. He does all kinds of wildly fun tricks, but he also wears protective gear and a helmet. God has protective gear for us to wear too. When we wear the gear, life is just safer!

Check out the pieces of armor mentioned in Ephesians 6:13-17:

> Therefore put on the full armor of God, so that when the day of evil comes, you may be able to stand your ground, and after you have done everything, to stand. Stand firm then, with the belt of truth buckled around your waist, with the breastplate of righteousness in place, and with your feet fitted with the readiness that comes from the gospel of peace. In addition to all this, take up the shield of faith, with which you can extinguish all the flaming arrows of the evil one. Take the helmet of salvation and the sword of the Spirit, which is the word of God.

The belt of truth. What is truth and where do you find it? Over and over Christ says in the Gospels, "I tell you the truth…" Jesus is the truth, and John explains that Jesus is also: "The Word became flesh and made his dwelling among us. We have seen his glory, the glory of the One and Only, who came from the Father, full of grace and truth" (John 1:14). The incarnate Word is truth, and the written Word He gave is truth: "Sanctify them by the truth; your word is truth" (John 17:17). The Word sets you free: "Then you will know the truth, and the truth will set you free" (John 8:32). When making decisions ask: "What is the truth in this situation?" Then pull out a concordance or use a Bible computer program to find the truth out about the issue.

The breastplate of righteousness. What is righteousness and how is it obtained? "For in the gospel a righteousness from God is revealed, a righteousness that is by faith from first to last, just as it is written: 'The righteous will live by faith'" (Romans 1:17). We become righteous as we live out our faith. "Abraham believed God, and it was credited to him as righteousness" (Romans 4:3). This righteousness is positioned in the armor to guard your heart.

The gospel of peace. Part of the armor of God is having our feet fitted with peace. "He [Jesus] came and preached peace to you who were far away and peace to those who were near" (Ephesians 2:17). I travel a lot. You may travel a lot or a little, but wherever our feet take us, we need to make sure we are sharing with others the good news that peace with God and each other is possible through the gift of His Son. When you are facing a decision, ask: "Will this decision treat everyone rightly? Will this decision bring peace or division?"

The shield of faith. Romans 10:17 says, "Consequently, faith comes from hearing the message, and the message is heard through the word of Christ." The Word! *Go back to people who know the Word and ask them their opinion.* Find people who will speak the word of truth into your life. Those words will shield you from making erratic decisions.

The helmet of salvation. Is the helmet of salvation any different? "Salvation is found in no one else, for there is no other name under heaven given to men by which we must be saved" (Acts 4:12). This verse is speaking of Jesus, the living Word. How does salvation take place?

> If you confess with your mouth, "Jesus is Lord," and believe in your heart that God raised him from the dead, you will be saved. For it is with your heart that you believe and are justified, and it is with your mouth that you confess and are saved. As the Scripture says, "Anyone who trusts in him will never be put to shame" (Romans 10:9-11).

The written Word tells the story of the living Word and we believe. The power is in the Word. If you are confused, ask yourself: "Am I listening to outside sources here? Am I placing more weight on the Word and people who know the Word, or am I trusting in the opinions of people without a personal faith in God?"

The sword of the Spirit. Hebrews 4:12 reminds us that, "For the word of God is living and active. Sharper than any double-edged sword, it penetrates even to dividing soul and spirit, joints and marrow; it judges the thoughts and attitudes of the heart." The sharpest sword is the Word. This is the hardest question of all: "Am I taking the easy way out just because the Word is making me uncomfortable?"

I'm sure you've got the picture. The power to obey is fueled by the Word of God. The more of God's Word we take in, the more likely we will live it out. But it isn't easy to keep the truth of the Bible central in your life. It takes work. My friend Robin and I were talking one day. We were both in the throes of midlife: caring for teens, caring for parents, caring for our spouses, caring for our own health, caring in leadership for some very important issues at the time. We both lamented how hard it was to maintain a sense of personal peace. "I know, Robin. It is all I can do to keep going back to the truth of the Word of God. It takes all my energy to make the bold strategic choice to obey and live out what I have learned all these years. The Bible is clear that life is a battle, and it is also clear that the way to victory is through the armor of God—which is just the truth of God. I guess if we were in war, in a real battle, we'd have to keep readjusting our armor and make sure we kept it on."

Robin replied, "Part of the armor of God are the sandals of peace. I guess we can encourage each other by asking, 'Are you keeping your shoes on?'" That simple friendship commitment has done so much to help both Robin and me maintain our peace through staying in the Word, memorizing it, and praying it over each other. To help us maintain our priority of being women who *decide* to live strategically, we ask each other regularly, "Got your shoes on?"

The Yield Sign

By asking, "What do you think, God?" I am spiritually counting to ten, and that momentary pause gives God the opportunity to lead instead of me forging ahead without consulting Him. Romans 6:13 clearly reveals the options and the results. "Neither yield ye your members as instruments of unrighteousness unto sin: but yield yourselves unto God, as those that are alive from the dead, and your members as instruments of righteousness unto God" (KJV). All we are asked to do is yield.

Yield means to voluntarily offer up something of value and put it under the control of another. Just as at a yield sign we pause and give over the right of way to the other car, yield means we pause, think through life, and then obey the law of the land. In our case, we yield our will to obedience to God.

It is now time for another math formula. If $A + B = C$ and $A + D = C$, then B and D must be the same. Abiding and yielding have the same impact—they make us *friends* of Christ.

People often ask me how I have accomplished so much in such a short amount of time. From the outside, people can see the 20 books that have been written in less than ten years. They see the travel schedule, and then they picture all the daily responsibilities that come with a home, children, and marriage. And when they read that for the majority of that time I was also a pastor's wife and ran *Masterful Living*, which for a time included a weekly radio show, they shake their heads in disbelief. They can't picture it. My schedule is just more visible. I think if many of us actually took the time to write down what we have accomplished—or need to—we'd all easily feel overwhelmed. Instead of being overwhelmed, as I said before, I simply choose to be obedient. I ask, "What's next, God?"

I could tell you to squeeze more time out of your day. I do, you do, we all do. We multitask, we buy fancy organizers and calendars, we file, we pile, we own phone message pads that record in triplicate. We buy personal organizers and computer software that keeps us on track, and some of us pay people to organize our life or we have personal assistants—and all these things work to help you find more time in your day—but what they don't do is tell you *how* to spend that time. Only God does that. Obedience is the key.

All I know is that when I abide in Christ, when I yield to His leading and try to do *what He wants me to when He wants me to,* it all works. It is like putting your hand in a glove. I am the glove. When I place myself on His hand, I move where He moves. A glove cannot move independently. Somehow, as long as I stay a glove and not try to be the hand, it all works. Moment by moment, it works.

Obedience keeps our thoughts on track, and our thoughts keep our actions on track, and, most importantly, I believe obedience keeps a woman's emotions on track! Laurie McIntyre, Director

202 The 10 Best Decisions a Woman Can Make

of Women at Elmbrook Church says, "Thoughts are the fore-runners to all of your actions."[3] By taking our thoughts captive as instructed in 2 Corinthians 10:5, we gain the ability to follow Jesus' lead. The word picture for taking thoughts captive is the picture of handcuffing them and throwing them into prison.[4] It is us deciding to arrest a thought. I usually say, "Don't go there!" and "What is the truth here?" Then I stand on the truth—that's why knowing the truth is so important. Truth is the prison guard of the mind. That's why the truth sets you free. Truth puts false thinking in prison.

When you have a pattern of not taking thoughts captive, your rational thinking patterns begin to erode. You can no longer think clearly. For example, these stories relay accounts of how people begin to think when they don't stay on truth and take their thoughts captive. A woman wrote to newspaper columnist Abigail Van Buren:

> Dear Abby,
>
> I am a twenty-three-year-old liberated woman who has been on the pill for two years. It's getting expensive, and I think my boyfriend should share half the cost, but I don't know him well enough to discuss money with him.

Knows him well enough for sex but not finances…hmmm… There's an adage that crooks are so stupid they end up getting caught. What do you think?

> A man in South Carolina walked into a local police station, dropped a bag of cocaine on the counter, informed the desk sergeant that it was substandard cut, and asked that the person who sold it to him be arrested immediately.

In Indiana a man walked up to a cashier at a grocery store and demanded all the money in the register. When the cashier handed him the loot, he fled—leaving his wallet on the counter.

A man decided to rob a bank. He handed a note to the teller and told her to fill up a bag with the money. After receiving the loot, he decided that the bag was too bulky to carry out of the bank without attracting attention. So he filled out a deposit slip and had the teller deposit the money into his bank account.

I'd say these folks have gone way too long without the guidance that comes from the truth! Discretion and clear thinking goes right out the window when the Word isn't in your life. Honesty becomes a hit-and-miss activity.

A man in our church designs computer software for the criminal justice system. One police officer relayed a story to our friend about a man he'd arrested and pulled into a lineup. Seems the crook who stole a woman's purse had said to the woman, "Give me that purse." The woman looking at the lineup was unsure if the culprit was there, so she asked the officer to have each of the men say, "Give me that purse." The first man in the lineup said, "I want your purse, give it to me!" and another man in the lineup stepped forward and said, "That's not what I said. I said, 'Hey lady, give me that purse!'" (At least he was honest—just a little too late!)

Bill and I have had some equally amazing things said to us. A woman, after smashing her husband's Rolex watch, said: "I don't understand why he is so hateful toward me."

A man who had slept with his girlfriend told us, "It must have been God's will that brought us together because the sex was so good. It felt so right."

"She looked at me funny, so I'm not going back to church." (Honest, it was really said!)

From a woman who'd had an affair with her best friend's husband and finally married him: "I just know it was God's will that I marry him because on the night of our wedding, there was a rainbow around the moon."

A new friend and I sat on the sidelines as our boys played soccer. She found out that my husband was a pastor, so she began to talk to me about spiritual issues. One day she brought up palm reading. I asked her why she had her palm read. She said she wanted help in knowing what to do in her future. I explained to her that God would love to do that for her. She said, "Oh, He did, when I got my palm read." I explained that God never tells us to do things that are opposite to what He says in His Word, and His Word says that fortune-tellers, tarot cards, and things like that are considered divination, and we are to have nothing to do with them. (See Deuteronomy18:10-14.)

"But it has to be okay with God. The palm reader prayed before she read my palm."

"But God is not schizophrenic. If He says don't do it, He means don't do it. It doesn't matter if the person uses Christian words or actions, it is not Christian. It isn't that we pray, it's to *whom we pray* that matters."

Stinkin' thinkin' sets in where there is no truth. The more we refuse to take our thoughts captive, the worse the thinking becomes. It's as though a callus develops over our heart and we are no longer sensitive to God's leading. Where there is a lack of truth, a sickness of thinking creeps in. On the other hand, where there is truth, there is also clarity and strategic, long-term, positive fruit.

Be Daring! It Pays

The first Christian books I ever read were poetry-prose written by Ann Kiemel Anderson. In one of her stories, she shared that her mother always told her, "It pays, it pays to follow Jesus." That phrase, "It pays," stuck in the back of my head as a freshman college student. Whenever I came to a place where it was emotionally challenging to follow Jesus, "It pays!" would echo in my heart and mind, and I'd gain the courage to obey.

It is easier to obey when I stand on the truth that God loves me and He has my best in mind at all times. Paul says, "If God is for us, who can be against us? He who did not spare his own Son, but gave him up for us all—how will he not also, along with him, graciously give us all things?" (Romans 8:31-32). David prayed in Psalm 17:8, knowing God would answer, "Keep me as the apple of your eye; hide me in the shadow of your wings." Jeremiah 31:3 promises, "The LORD appeared to us in the past, saying: 'I have loved you with an everlasting love; I have drawn you with loving-kindness.'" And in Psalm 32:8 we are assured: "I will instruct you and teach you in the way you should go; I will counsel you and watch over you." Believing that God loves me draws me into obedience.

When I was dating Bill, I came to a crossroad in my relationship with him and with God. I had made a list of the kind of person I wanted to someday marry by listing traits I saw in the New Testament in Christ and His disciples. It was a list of internal character qualities: loving, respectful of women, a good listener, kind and compassionate. Bill fit the list. Our hearts and plans were running in the same direction, but because we were allowing God to rework our dating patterns, we were both in new territory emotionally. One week in my quiet times, I became impressed with the fact that on the following weekend when I saw Bill, I would need to know where I stood on areas of physical boundaries. I knew my past pattern of letting the guy take the lead wasn't very wise, so I let God take the lead this time. I studied and saw the verses that backed up my decision to remain a virgin. But I also

saw a pattern, and as I prayed I became convinced that our physical relationship needed to progress forward only after tangible
measures of commitment. When God said, "I love you," He
demonstrated it! I thought that was a good principle.

That weekend Bill and I sat on a rock in the sunshine and talked
for hours as we watched the ocean. It was one of the best days of
my life. I felt so cherished, so loved, so wanted. Bill had a list of
questions he wanted to ask me about, and they mostly concerned
our physical boundaries. How far did we think God wanted us
to go and when? We navigated our conversation through, holding hands, hugging, and walking arm in arm. We'd already decided
God was clear about no sex before marriage—it was all the stuff
in between we were concerned and confused about now. I saw on
the list "kissing" and I knew God had prepared me for that weekend.

But Bill stopped short and didn't ask me about it. He took me
to my friends' apartment where I was staying to get ready for our
evening date. And that evening was magical too. A quiet romantic fondue dinner and a walk through the downtown district over
bridges and creeks and under gaslights on a foggy night. We walked
and talked, and talked and walked, and I was getting cold, so Bill
wrapped his arms around me and tucked me into his car to take
me back to my friends. He stopped at his place first, and I went
in with him. It was there he asked, "Pam, can I kiss you?"

My body wanted to rush into his arms and let him kiss me
over and over again, but the Holy Spirit inside me reminded me
of my quiet time conversations with God that I had journaled all
week.

"Bill, I want to say yes, but I can't. You see, I've wrecked all
my past relationships because I haven't watched over this area of
my life very well. I value my relationship with you too much to
say yes. So until you're ready to commit to me as the person you'd

like to marry, then I have to say no. If you'd like to kiss me on the cheek that would be okay…so…no. I care for you, but I care for God more…so….” I trailed off as he stared at me in silence. He brushed my tearstained cheek with fingertips for a brief moment, took my hand, and drove me home in utter silence for 20 minutes.

I told him again at the door what a wonderful day I had had with him and how much I loved being with him, and he mumbled something about picking me up for breakfast at 8 A.M.

I opened the door and burst into tears. My girlfriends rushed toward me. “What's wrong? What's wrong?”

I told them the story and said, “I am so afraid I might have said goodbye to the best man I've ever had in my life. I just knew God had been preparing me and I had a choice, Bill's will or God's will in my life. I had to choose God.”

One of my friends tried to comfort me, “Pam, we all know Bill, and he wants God's best in his life and in yours. You have to trust his character. If he really is the godly man he appears to be, he'll handle this.”

Another said, “You have to trust God. After all, He got you into this thing!”

So the group of us prayed together. They slept and I lay awake a while longer, wondering what the new day would bring.

Bill was smiling when he picked me up in the morning. He drove me to a beautiful scenic precipice where we could see the bright early sun dance across the ocean waves. “Pam, I didn't say anything last night because I didn't know what to say. I've never been in the presence of a woman as committed to God as you are. Just being with you strengthens my walk with God. Pam, I was hurt and embarrassed last night. I felt like I should have been the one who protected our purity; that's why I was quiet. But I want you to know I totally agree with you. You are the best thing that has ever happened to me, and I don't want our relationship to crumble because we didn't watch over our sexuality. I won't play games with your heart. When I am ready to marry you, then I will ask to kiss you."

A few months later, at the same beach house where Bill first asked me for a kiss, he bent on his knee, sang a song he wrote especially for me, and then asked me to marry him. Of course I said, "Yes!" Then he asked, "May I kiss you?"

"Yes!!!" And it was a kiss worth waiting for. Bill and I often reflect back on that daring decision to obey God in the very difficult place of our sexuality. We have come to see that our choice to wait forced us to find other ways to communicate our feelings and our love. Because of this our romantic relationship was strengthened and our sexual relationship in marriage has always been very rich and exciting and fulfilling—even almost 25 years later! And now we have an international marriage ministry! One of our books on marriage, *Men Are Like Waffles—Woman Are Like Spaghetti* (Harvest House), is translated in over six languages! We are often guests on national and international radio and television shows, even mainstream talk shows that are beamed to billions of people! Dare to obey—it pays!

I Dare You to Jump!

Our decision landed in a gray area, one not specifically detailed in Scripture. All we did is listen to the Holy Spirit whisper that God wanted us to apply verses that encourage a pure heart and a pure mind. Because of our knowledge of the Bible and because our hearts were attuned to God's leading in our lives, when God spoke to my heart, it was not ambiguous. We heard loud and clear what the Holy Spirit wanted us to do—we only had to choose to obey. It felt like a risk, but that is what being daring feels like! It was a risk well worth it. Obedience is trust in the *person* of God. The key question, the big decision point, is then, "How well do I know God? Do I really trust Him with all my life? And if I trust Him, what is He asking me to do so my life reflects a life of character?

Just like a child standing on the side of a pool, your loving Father in heaven is saying, "Jump! Jump to me! You can trust Me! I know what's best for you!" Dare to be different. Dare to obey. Now, jump!

Decision Points

Is there a decision you are needing clarity on? Try one of the big picture methods and see if you can gain God's perspective on the issue.

Is there an issue that is causing you to have a difficult time obeying God? As you look back over your life, do you see any pivotal decisions when obedience made the difference? Are there pivotal moments you wished you'd obeyed? Try to list five or six times you know obedience made the difference in the course your life took. Remember, God does have your best interests in mind!

Find a verse that speaks of God's care to your heart and memorize it. Are you feeling emotionally distraught over a circumstance? Ask yourself: "What is the truth about this situation? What is my part? What is God's part?" Ruth Graham, wife of evangelist Billy Graham, says, "You do the possible and trust God with the impossible."[5] God cares more about you finding and walking in His will than even you do! He will lead you. My favorite verse that shows God's caring guidance is Isaiah 31:21, "Whether you turn to the right or to the left, your ears will hear a voice behind you, saying, 'This is the way; walk in it.'" The key is to have ears to hear the whisper of the Holy Spirit and a heart that will follow.

Do you have a decision to make? Is it a hard one and you aren't sure what to do? Do you know someone who really seems to know God well? Make an appointment. Ask your spiritual advisor to pray for you and give you verses that relate to your decision. Then set aside time to reflect on how God wants you to obey what you are reading.

Maybe you know exactly when and where your life went offtrack. Tell God you are sorry and you want some help to walk in obedience now. If you can, go back and make things right. If it is too late to set things right, then at least go back and apologize to anyone your actions might have hurt. It will feel risky, but remember, God will be holding your hand and walking with you all the way. The right choice is always the obedience choice.

$\mathcal{D}$ecide to $\mathcal{L}$eave a $\mathcal{L}$egacy

Giving Your Life to What Matters Most

$\mathcal{I}$ was looking forward to this trip to Oklahoma. My father had been raised in the state and coming to speak here felt a little like coming home. After I landed, two leaders met me in the airport. I immediately knew this trip was going to be different from many of the others. They had an excitement that was contagious. I sensed God's favor was with this group as we chatted over lunch. No one ate much lunch because the more we talked, the less important the food became. After lunch they asked me if I wanted to stop at a local historical monument, and I answered in the affirmative.

The monument was the site of the April 19, 1995, bombing of the federal building in Oklahoma City. A chain-link fence guarded the site of the now-leveled building that has since been turned into a memorial. The fence was covered for blocks and blocks with memorabilia. (I learned later that there were warehouses full of gifts from the outpouring of the public's hearts.) As I walked that fence, I knew I would never again be the same woman. On the fence were spontaneous gifts of people who had come to the site. Hundreds and hundreds of teens must have taken off their WWJD?[1] bracelets. There were T-shirts from clubs, youth groups, and churches with signatures and verses written on them. There were Christmas and birthday presents meant for the victims who had died in the bombing. Wreaths with eulogies and poems and pictures of the victims decorated the somber fence like

Christmas lights wrapped around a mile-long gravestone. Bibles opened to a specific comforting verse were affixed as beacons of hope. Hymnals with song pages like "It Is Well with My Soul" dotted the fence line. At one end of the memorial stands a towering white sculpture of Jesus, head bowed, and the plaque at His feet simply reads "Jesus wept" (John 11:35). That weekend as I talked, wept, read, and prayed with those dear women of Edmond, Oklahoma, I realized they had one advantage over most of the rest of the world. They had ordered priorities. Coming face-to-face with the brevity of life had forever changed them.

In today's world, we all have come to grips with the brevity of life. Two boys walked into a high school in Littleton, Colorado, on April 20, 1999, and began shooting. Two planes crashed into the World Trade Center towers on September 11, 2001. I live in San Diego, and 2003 saw us weekly waving goodbye to members of the military who have given their lives to keep us free and to bring liberty to those held in bondage. Even as I write this, the largest fire in California history has swept over my hometown, and burned in the ashes are the lives of more than a dozen people.

It's Life and Death

It was a normal workday that April morning in 1995. At 9:02 coffee cups were in hand or on the desks of many of the workers in the building. A majority of the people in the building were women, many single mothers, trying their best to provide for their families. Some of them took advantage of the day care center on the building's lower level.

At 9:02 A.M. a bomb exploded and lives stopped. All the survivors, those inside and those outside, had to make a choice about what was really important, what was indeed significant, and then they proceeded ahead. For most it was a split-second decision. Years of moral lessons heard in church, at home, and in the community ran to the forefront of their minds. *People* matter most.

Soon signs sprung up around the city, declaring a source of hope and encouragement. One read, *God is our refuge and strength* (Psalm 46:1), and another simply read, *Good will overcome evil.*

How were we to know that just a few short years later, on September 11, 2001, thousands of innocent lives would be lost again because of evil. When the Twin Towers fell, our hearts fell; but when we learned what police officers, firefighters, and the passengers of Flight 93 did to try to save lives, our hearts soared with hope. On drastic days, priorities become clear: save *people.* The World Trade Center housed some of the world's most prominent and powerful organizations and businesses, but those important papers seemed as meaningless as the confetti they became in light of the need to rescue *people.*

Children of the Light

How can good overcome evil? The idea of being light and the idea of being God's temple are connected. Just as the temple in Jerusalem was the symbol of God's holiness, righteousness, and truth, so we too, as the church, are the representation of God's righteousness on earth. Paul expresses this idea when he says, "For you were once darkness, but now you are light in the Lord. Live as children of light" (Ephesians 5:8).

Just as light emanated from the temple and proclaimed the glory of God, God's light emanates from us and proclaims His transforming power. In so doing, our lives expose the darkness of unrighteous living.

Living together as a body, we build one another up and grow toward maturity. As family, we find our attitudes and values changed as love becomes the touchstone of our lives. As God's temple, we find our lives taking on a holiness which exposes evil for what it is. Living together as a holy temple means rejecting dark things and building our commitment to goodness, righteousness, and truth.[2]

How does the church, a gathering of people who love God, expose evil? By mounting a crusade or picketing? Hardly. Evil is exposed by providing an example of righteousness.

Paul put it this way: "Everything exposed by the light becomes visible, for it is light that makes everything visible" (Ephesians 5:13-14). As children of light, we reveal darkness for what it is. In the light shed by the holiness of God's people, evil is revealed as evil.[3]

So what did the temple look like when God's glory took up residence? First Kings 8:10-11 explains what it looked like when the glory of the Lord resided in the temple Solomon built: "When the priests withdrew from the Holy Place, the cloud filled the temple of the LORD. And the priests could not perform their service because of the cloud, for the glory of the LORD filled his temple." Second Chronicles 7:1-3 adds to the picture and says, "Fire came down from heaven and consumed the burnt offering and the sacrifices, and the glory of the LORD filled the temple...When all the Israelites saw the fire coming down and the glory of the LORD above the temple, they knelt on the pavement with their faces to the ground, and they worshiped and gave thanks to the LORD, saying, 'He is good; his love endures forever.'"

The prophet Ezekiel tries to explain what the glory of the Lord looked like to him, "Like the appearance of a rainbow in the clouds on a rainy day, so was the radiance around him. This was the appearance of the likeness of the glory of the LORD. When I saw it, I fell facedown, and I heard the voice of one speaking" (Ezekiel 1:28). He notes later, "Then the glory of the LORD rose from above the cherubim and moved to the threshold of the temple. The cloud filled the temple, and the court was full of the radiance of the glory of the LORD" (Ezekiel 10:4). That is the picture God is trying to explain when He says we are children of the light. His glory, revealed through our lives, will have a dramatic impact on people.

You are children of the light seems to not say what we should do or be, but rather *who we are* because we dwell in His presence.

His presence has a natural effect on us—and on the world around us.

There are times when we can ponder, plan, and think out our actions and reactions, but this title of *children of the light* seems to lead us to the conclusion that when we are in Christ, we *are* different. We have radically different reactions, even when there is no time to think, no time to wonder, no time to rationalize, and no time to prepare a flowchart or draft a business plan. "Therefore be careful how you walk, not as unwise men, but as wise, making the most of your time, because the days are evil" (Ephesians 5:15-16 NASB).

God adds to the picture when He says, "You are all sons of the light and sons of the day. We do not belong to the night or to the darkness. So then, let us not be like others, who are asleep, but let us be alert and self-controlled" (1 Thessalonians 5:5-6). *You are sons of the light, sons of the day.* You and I are to be alert and in control of our senses.

The Heartbeat of an Ambassador

Driving tests are designed to examine a person's reaction time to see if he or she is able to avoid obstacles and stop in time to avoid calamity. The doctor tests your reaction when he taps your knee to see if your reflexes are working. As children of the light, our natural reflex is to walk in the light. Those not in fellowship with God are drawn to darkness. Those connected to Christ are drawn toward a life that emanates light.

When we walk in the light, our heart wants to obey. We have an intrinsic yearning to serve. The higher the stakes, the more likely we are to want to obey and serve. We trust God, so we serve Him. I think it is because when we come to know God personally, our role is changed from that of a citizen of society to an ambassador. Just as ambassadors seek to reconcile countries, we seek to reconcile people to God. Because we have a heart for reconciliation, our priorities shift. We can see what is imperative. People become the priority.

"We are therefore Christ's ambassadors, as though God were making his appeal through us. We implore you on Christ's behalf: Be reconciled to God" (2 Corinthians 5:20). The imperative is made clear because God's appeal is going out through us. *You are an ambassador!* God is offering reconciliation to Himself. When we look at people, we should have the same heart as the people at the site of the Oklahoma City bombing, or the same thoughts as the captain and crew on the sinking *Titanic:* How many can be rescued? As many as we possibly can. Who is in eminent peril? We need to get to them first. This is the heartbeat of an ambassador for Christ.

Ambassadors who serve in foreign countries realize they will never totally feel comfortable in the host country because it is not their homeland. The same is true of us. If we truly have the heart of an ambassador, we will realize that our citizenship is in heaven (see Philippians 3:20).

Ambassadors also seek to learn the language and the culture of their host country so they can be more effective. Ambassadors want what is best for the people of their host country—what is physically, emotionally, socially, and politically best, but primarily what is spiritually best. Proverbs 13:17 explains the result of a heart that wants the best for the host people: "A faithful ambassador brings health" (NKJV). Ambassadors give what is needed, when it is needed.

A Salute from Heaven

I was preparing for a flight to Germany and overwhelmed by feelings of complete inadequacy. I had been booked to speak at this event for two years. It was a simple leadership training event to me when I first booked it. I was excited and confident, but now my prayers became frantic as I begged God to somehow work through me to bring hope and help to an audience I felt so unworthy to address: the wives of military service men who just a day before had packed up their spouses and sent them into war in the Middle East. (I mentioned this incident in an earlier chapter. Here is a bit more.)

Lord, what will I say? How can I even begin? I pulled up my e-mail to create the "I'll be out of town" auto reply and saw that a friend had e-mailed me the perfect beginning. Here's an excerpt of the "Stand Up for America Rally" speech by Beth Chapman:

> I'm here tonight because men and women of the United States military have given their lives for my freedom. I am not here tonight because Sheryl Crow, Rosie O'Donnell, Martin Sheen, George Clooney, Jane Fonda or Phil Donahue, sacrificed their lives for me.
>
> If my memory serves me correctly, it was not movie stars or musicians, but the United States military who fought on the shores of Iwo Jima, the jungles of Vietnam, and the beaches of Normandy...
>
> On December 7, 1941, there are no records of movie stars treading the blazing waters of Pearl Harbor. On September 11, 2001, there are no photos of movie stars standing as "human shields" against the debris and falling bodies descending from the World Trade Center. There were only policemen and firemen—underpaid civil servants who gave their all with nothing expected in return...
>
> Throughout the course of history, this country has remained free, not because of movie stars and liberal activists, but because of brave men and women who...lay down their lives so that we all may live in freedom. After

all—"Greater love hath no man than this, that he lay down his life for his friend."

Thousands and thousands of white headstones dot Arlington cemetery. How many of their names do you know? Ambassadors for Christ aren't always well known—in fact most are unknown to the masses but applauded by the heavens. Christian women, believing God for freedom, worked behind the Berlin Wall until the fall of Communism came. Women, some with newfound faith, fanned the flame of hope through underground churches in China, the Sudan, and other countries hostile against Christianity. Women, believing all people are created equal, carried the love of Christ in South Africa, a country torn in two by apartheid. It was "church women" who first ignited the suffrage movement that garnered women the right to vote. Women who loved God were those who authored the Declaration of Sentiments that was read in Seneca Falls, New York, in the Wesleyan Church. These women are ambassadors who are at great risk at times. While writing this book, I received an e-mail prayer request from a European mission:

> There is a beautiful 15-year-old girl named Saleema in Pakistan who is a Christian. She converted her close friend, 14. This youngster was so excited about Christianity that she told her parents, and they killed her! It looks like the 15-year-old is to be publicly executed. We need to send up prayer for this child to give her the strength and resolve to deal with whatever happens to her.

Humble Beginnings

Ambassadors can also be raised up from obscure beginnings. On October 31, 1896, in a Philadelphia slum, a 12-year-old rape victim gave birth alone. The baby might not have made it, but a neighbor heard the infant's cries and came to the rescue. The small child later was taken to church, where she learned to sing. At age five, she gave her first performance in front of that tiny congregation. Ethel ran wild in the streets, practically raising herself. She traveled with a black vaudeville group before her jazz vocals led her to the famous Cotton Club, where she introduced the song, "Stormy Weather," which she said was a picture of her life. Nicknamed Mama Stringbean, Ethel Waters became the first black radio star and then a famed movie actress. But the songs of her youth clung to her soul. In 1957 at a Billy Graham crusade, she rededicated her life to God. In the following years, her theme song became "His Eye Is on the Sparrow," and she traveled with the Billy Graham crusade, as a singing ambassador of hope, proclaiming to millions that God's love can overcome anything life dishes out.[4]

Being an ambassador is a calling. Os Guinness in his book *The Call* says, "First and foremost we are called to Someone (God), not to something (such as motherhood, politics, or teaching), or to somewhere (such as the inner city or Outer Mongolia).[5]...There is no calling unless there is a Caller."[6] Romans 1:6-7 clearly supports our call to the *person* of God. "And you also are among those who are called to belong to Jesus Christ." *You are called!*

His calling is personal. Jesus called the Twelve by name. God came to Abram, Jacob, and Moses as individuals. The Lord came to Ananias and to Saul. God calls you as a person. He knows you and He calls you.

His calling is permanent. "For God's gifts and his call are irrevocable" (Romans 11:29).

His calling brings purpose. Jesus designated twelve apostles, and then He gave them power, authority, and a plan. The Holy Spirit said to the early church leaders, "Set apart Barnabas and Saul for the work to which I have called them" (Acts 13:2). Paul was called to be an apostle (Romans 1:1). We are called, and then God gives us our purpose.

His calling leads to a principled life. Paul's prayer in 2 Thessalonians 1:11 gives us a clue on the lifestyle of a called one: "With this in mind, we constantly pray for you, that our God may count you worthy of his calling, and that by his power he may fulfill every good purpose of yours and every act prompted by your faith." What a wonderful partnership! By God's power He will fulfill every good purpose of *yours* and every act prompted by *your* faith. We can experience such freedom in being called. It seems that the only prerequisite is that God counts us worthy. So let's look at what we are called to. You and I are called: to come after Christ, to take up our cross and follow Christ;[7] according to God's purpose;[8] to be free;[9] to one hope;[10] peace;[11] a holy life;[12] to receive the promised eternal inheritance;[13] to suffer;[14] to inherit a blessing;[15] to be the servant of all.[16]

It seems that one who truly lives out her calling has the internal strength and wisdom to climb the ladder of success quite easily. She will have purpose, freedom, hope, peace, holiness, an inheritance, a blessing, perseverance, and a positive *servant* attitude.

After 9/11, leaving Shea Stadium after a New York Mets game one summer afternoon, an eight-year-old boy with a baseball glove approached a policeman who was directing traffic and asked him to sign his glove. "Don't you want a ballplayer's autograph? Why a cop's?"

The boy responded, "Because you helped save the world."

When we have a servant's heart, God can use us. Each of us, serving next to each other, shoulder to shoulder, will move His causes forward. We become living stones, small acts of service laying a foundation expressing the love of Christ: "You also, like living stones, are being built into a spiritual house to be a holy priesthood, offering spiritual sacrifices acceptable to God through Jesus Christ" (1 Peter 2:5). The words *spiritual house* are the same used by Jesus to Peter when Christ said he was building His church on the rock. Each of us are a stone in the spiritual house God is building. *You are a living stone* right now!

God gives three other word pictures to show the value of a servant's heart. In 1 Corinthians 3:9, Paul says, "For we are God's fellow workers; you are God's field, God's building." *God's fellow workers* means we are coworkers of God, thus giving our work dignity, no matter what it is we do. God is the major partner in the enterprise of each life, but He lets us work with Him.

God's field is the picture of our servant role. The field is help-less until the sun shines and until the farmer sows seed and tends to the needs of the crop. I grew up on a farm. My job each summer was to tend our garden. The first few days were the most diffi-cult. We had to rototill the hard, compact dirt and then plant the seed, water, and weed. The ground became more and more valu-able the more time we invested in it. We are the same way. The more time God invests in us, the more usable we become.

God's building is an architectural picture.[17] When Bill was completing his education, he worked as an architectural drafts-man, and I worked to help him. No one knew the drawings had walls colored by me. It didn't really matter as long as all the struc-tural specifications were accurate. The same is true all through the building process. Do you know the names of all the carpen-ters, plumbers, cabinetmakers, cement workers, and so on who built the home you live in? Probably not. In the same way, God is saying life still has purpose, even when you don't get the credit for the work.

What Is Needed?

Clayton Hoskinson, an investigator for the Oklahoma Depart-ment of Human Services, was directing traffic the day of the bombing. By mid-morning a fine mist had become a driving rain. He was cold, wet, and miserable. An old car, barely running, pulled into the intersection. The driver cracked his window. "Is this where I'm supposed to drop off the boots?" he asked.

"I had no information about a need for boots. The man had just heard a plea on the radio for steel-toed boots. I told him that we could put the boots with other items, and he rolled down his window and handed me the boots. In the car with him were a woman, an infant, and two small children. Taking the boots, I immediately noticed they felt warm on the inside. Looking back into the car I saw the man was wearing no shoes.

"Are these your boots?" I asked.

"Yes." He nodded.

"Sir, no one expects you to give up your own boots," I said as I attempted to hand them back through the window.

With a tear in his eye, he said, "There are people in there who need them worse than I do."[18]

Steven Davis, a corporal with the Oklahoma City fire department had ripped his boots while digging for survivors. He was issued a new pair of boots and inside he found a note: "God bless the man who wears these boots, that he may be strong in his search for life." His wife, Tami, framed the note and each time he sees it he thinks, "God bless you too, my friend."[19]

Not About You

When you have a view from heaven, you place people in front of profit. In Oklahoma City, stores donated items off their shelves. One government worker came to town with 55 cents in his pocket, stayed for over two weeks, and in his pocket the day he left was the same 55 cents. The people of the city had taken care of every need out of gratitude for his service and leadership. When the television stations needed a broadcast location, the owner of a computer store donated his store site, shut down his business, and refused the lucrative payment the network offered because he didn't want to profit over others' pain. My luncheon friends had spouses who were doctors, and those in the medical field worked round the clock for months. Everyone pitched in and did whatever needed to be done.

But the strongest picture of a true ambassador, a real servant, was the constant stream of brave firefighters running into the towers of the World Trade Center the morning of September 11. I was in my car a few days later, listening to talk radio and trying to process the tragedy that had shaken up an entire country. With the toppling of the Twin Towers, the nation's confidence was challenged, people's security was rattled, and priorities were reshuffled. A man called the radio show I was tuned into and summed up for me everything that it meant to be a part of America in a time like this.

He related the story of one of his best friends who had been working at the World Trade Center. He was one of the fortunate ones low enough in the building to be evacuated. As he was walking down the stairway to get out of harm's way, he was passing firemen and other rescue professionals who were going up the stairs to save the lives of those trapped in the building. He said he looked them in the eyes and realized they were not planning on coming out. They were going to perform their jobs and rescue as many people as possible, even though they knew it would probably cost them their lives.

He then went on: "People say they are afraid of the enemy because they proved that on 9/11 they were willing to pay any price to further their cause. I, however, no longer fear them. I have seen real heroes that I can point out to my children. I saw these firemen who were willing to pay any price to maintain our freedom and save lives, and I knew we could never be defeated."

What do people see in your eyes? What price are you willing to pay to bring people the hope and help they need? What are you willing to sacrifice to bring the love of God to *people* who desperately need it? Are you willing to be a hero of the faith? Edmund Burke said, "The only thing necessary for the triumph of evil is for good men to do nothing."

In Philippians 2:4-5 and 8, we are challenged: "Each of you should look not only to your own interests, but also to the interests of others. Your attitude should be the same as that of Christ Jesus…he humbled himself and became obedient to death—even death on a cross!"

In Littleton, after the Columbine tragedy, numerous high school students came to faith in Christ. After 9/11, renewed faith and respect for God swept the nation. For a time, everyone sang, "God Bless America." In Oklahoma, a revival has taken place. Churches, brimming with people, have built bigger buildings and hired staff because each person is taking the message of hope to those they know. And there is a spirit of sacred somberness that permeates relationships. I experienced it firsthand on my trip to Edmond.

There is a singular focus that has captured the hearts of the people I met. In their ears ring verses like "What good is it for a man to gain the whole world, yet forfeit his soul?" (Mark 8:36); "Just as man is destined to die once, and after that to face judgment" (Hebrews 9:27); and "Salvation is found in no one else, for there is no other name under heaven given to men by which we must be saved" (Acts 4:12).

It is important to remember God doesn't force people to come to Him. People have a choice. I have heard excuses before, "Oh, I don't want to know a God who could send people to hell." God doesn't send us to hell—we send ourselves there. We choose to live apart from Him or we choose to give our heart to Him. For example, if I were married to a bad man, and we were in an argument, and I was afraid for my life and wanted to leave, if that man blocked off the door, that is a crime. It is called blocking egress. I could dial 911 and he would be arrested. God doesn't block our egress. God is a gentleman. He doesn't force Himself on anyone, but He instead offers a love relationship. The choice is ours to have a relationship with Him. It is a choice that each person alive deserves to hear about. But how will they hear if no one tells them, writes them, or gives them information? That is our clear call as ambassadors. Get people the 411 on God!

New Lenses

In the races for the hearts and souls of humankind, many things pale in importance when looked at through the lens of eternity. The bathroom that needs a fresh coat of paint falls further down the list when you look at people in your neighborhood through "forever" eyes. The imperfect husband, flaws and all, looks pretty terrific when you consider the alternative of never having him around again. Washing dishes and diapers and driving children to activities that build their lives become holy acts in light of eternity.

Bill Bright, the founder of Campus Crusade for Christ, considered any time he was with someone more than a few minutes as a divine appointment. We have all eternity to praise God, sing to Him, and fellowship with believers, but we only have this short life to tell others about Him and the plan He offers to them. God could have taken each of us directly to heaven the moment we received His grace and love, but instead He chose to leave us here. The stakes are high in this game of life. Each of us will stand before God and give an account. His main priority on that day will be, "Do you know Me? Have you accepted My Son into your life as a payment for your imperfections?" Millions and millions of people have yet to hear the good news of God's great love in a way they can understand and accept. We are His voice to a lost and dying world. Today might seem like any other ordinary day, but so did April 19, 1995, in Oklahoma City. So did September 11, 2001, in New York City.

Since college I have tried to make all my decisions based on a single question, "What will this do to bring people to Jesus?" Sometimes getting a van has been a strategic move so that I can drive more children and teens to events to hear about God or grow in Christ. We built our home with evangelism in mind—a larger living room and kitchen for hospitality. But other times I know deep in my heart that it is me who wants Waverly print wallpaper, not God. It is me who desires a new outfit when God wants a missionary wife to have that money. As I weigh out my motives now, thousand of faces from Oklahoma City, the World Trade Center, the halls of a high school in scenic Colorado, flash across my mind.

And the face of my friend Diane. Diane and I were both on the gymnastics team, the cheer squad, and in dance club. Often, if I wasn't with my sister, Deney, I was with Diane.

At my 20-year high school reunion, the names of all those who had died in my class were read. Among those were a young man I had dated, one my sister had dated, and a friend from dance class. I recognized nearly everyone on the list, and I remembered the moments when God had prompted me to relate to each my personal story of faith.

I remember the excuses well: *God, what if they reject me? What if I lose them as a friend? What if they ask me questions and I don't know the answers? What if they laugh? What if they just aren't interested?* I asked Him all those questions—and more. I longed for a plausible excuse not to share my faith. I tried the *I'm too busy, God,* the *I don't know enough, God,* and the spiritual, *I'm sure someone else would do a better job, God.* I even tried the *I'm not sure it's the right time, God* excuse, but that still, small voice kept nudging me forward. In each case I said yes to Him and stepped out and shared my story of how He had radically redeemed my life and the hope He offered each of these friends. One by one I talked to them. Some responded right away and some didn't. All I know is that God asked and I nodded and obeyed.

God asked me to share my faith with my cheerleading friends from high school. Only a couple came to my house that day. I felt as though I'd failed Him somehow. Diane had called and said she wanted to come but had to work, so I set up a lunch appointment with her. Over lunch I shared Christ the only way I knew how— I read her the *Four Spiritual Laws*. Diane wanted to make a choice to have Christ come into her life that day, but she was afraid. She was living with a young man, and she didn't think he'd like her anymore if she got religious. When I explained it wasn't a religion, it was a relationship, she said she'd think about it. And she was true to her word.

I'd taken Diane to church with me a few times in high school, and on and off during those early college years we connected. Sometimes she'd come to a special event at church, sometimes we'd just talk. We were at each other's weddings (she married that young man she had been living with).

But a series of moves in and out of town for each of us made our relationship hit-and-miss over the next several years. At the ten-year reunion we connected again. Her first marriage had ended, and I could tell she was hurting. She was out of a job and pregnant with no husband in sight. We talked for quite a while that night. "Diane, God has a wonderful plan for your life, and I'd be glad to help you find it. God loves you. He wants the best for you, but you need to take the step and ask Him into your life."

She had a lot of questions, so we began to write back and forth. She was a single mom trying to get her life back on track. I sent a baby gift when her little one arrived and a card when she got a new job. She wanted to know more about God, so I sent her things I thought could help her make the decision to come to the loving God who had created her. Then the letters suddenly stopped. I wrote and my letters were returned by the post office. I wondered if I had done something wrong.

At the next reunion, I found out why the letters stopped. Diane had been driving home after a long day at her new job. She drove her car off an exit embankment. Two small children were now motherless.

I told my brother about my friend Diane after the reunion that night. Bret pointed to the late-night news. Pictures of Princess Diana's crumpled car blazed across the television. Diane and Diana each had a calendar jammed with important activities and plans, but the most important choice they needed to have made was a choice to give God the reins of their hearts. Only He knows their choice for sure.

But on the night of my 20-year reunion, I experienced something I will never forget. I felt as though my life had pleased God. The fragmented pieces fell into place. As the names of my dead classmates were read in a moment of silence, I was humbled that I, a woman who began life as a trembling, insecure child, had been so transformed that at a point in time, when it mattered most, I'd said yes to God and shared Him with others.

I wish I could say I always say yes when I feel that nudge from eternity. But I do say yes much more often because those classmates' names and those faces and stories from a chain-link fence in Oklahoma City are etched on my heart and my mind. I believe that God wants to help pull the pieces of our lives together so we don't feel so fragmented and stressed. But I *know* that the most important piece, a corner piece that sets the puzzle in place and helps it all fall together, is how my heart responds to life when I place the grid of eternity over the faces I pass each day. When I look at people and life's tasks through *forever eyes*, I gain perspective and clarity. Things that I thought were so important, so vital, fall into the background. Other times, things that at first glance seem insignificant can grow in significance under the microscope of heaven.

There was a woman, new to our congregation, who battled cancer for many years. Marcia was sick the entire time I knew her. I went to see her in a tiny condo. I knew she continued to work, even through the pain. Her world seemed small. When she passed away, I thought, *I should really go to her service. There might not be that many people there. It is even more painful for the family when few people come to a funeral.* So although I didn't know Marcia well, I went. As I drove into the parking lot, I had trouble finding a space. As the funeral proceeded, my husband opened up the mike for people in the congregation to share. Person after person streamed to the front to share how one woman, a woman who smiled through the pain of cancer every day for over ten years, had touched their lives. Most had never had a spiritual conversation until they had met her. But Marcia listened. She listened to crazy questions, she listened to breaking hearts, she listened to some people who may never have been listened to before—and she had made a difference.

Heart Ablaze

Every fall in California we have hot dry winds called the Santa Ana winds. When they blow for any length of time, the risk of brush fire goes up. One evening I noticed that a brush fire that had started earlier that day was now cropping the hilltops that surround our church building. It was still miles away, so I went inside to set up for a Bible study I was leading. I had been watching the news all day. People and animals were being evacuated from all the cities around ours. The wind had been carrying the fire away from our city—until that evening.

I again stepped outside to survey the situation as the women began to arrive for the study. We quickly gathered together and decided that what God wanted us to do that night was not study the Bible, but put it into action. I took our church phone directory and we divided up names so that we could call and check on those living in the area, especially our senior church members. We were to inform them of the wind shift, offer evacuation help, and information on emergency shelters. Most of the women at the study also offered their homes. I paged my husband, and our church soon became an emergency evacuation shelter. Bill manned the shelter, aiding anyone in need all night long, while I manned the phone like a dispatcher, relaying information to families who had been separated and friends checking on loved ones in the area. Then every 20 minutes or so, I called a few friends who lived at the ridge across a small lake from the fire. And I prayed. Neither Bill nor I slept that night, but we didn't care. People were safe, and that was all that mattered.

As we drove and surveyed the damage the fire had made, Bill and I couldn't help but notice an amazing site. Two wooden crosses survived the blaze when houses, brush, and trees had not. They seemed to be a beacon of hope and guidance to our community, a reminder of what really matters most in life: *people and their relationship to God.*

The Gift

It was 3 A.M. in Oklahoma City and cold, windy, and wet as Police Lieutenant Jim Spearman stood at the perimeter of the bombing site. Because the weather was so bad, the leaders of the search and rescue team were taking turns standing guard outside. Jim noticed three people standing just north of the barricade: a teenage boy, a younger girl, and a woman. He thought it was very strange that on a night like this and at that time anyone would be out and about. He approached the group. The boy walked forward and asked Jim if his younger sister could talk to him. The woman prompted the little girl, who appeared to be about nine. The little girl held a well-worn teddy bear and asked, "Could you give this to one of those babies in the hospital?"

The woman explained that the little girl hadn't been sleeping well since the bombing and was very concerned about the child victims. She had awakened about an hour before and asked if she could go to the bomb site. The bear had been given to her for her first birthday.

Jim told her he would take the teddy bear to the Salvation Army post and they would make sure that one of the children in the hospital got it. The little girl held out her beloved teddy bear. Jim leaned down and asked, "What's your name?"

Her reply: "That's not important."[20]

Lord, give me the heart of this little girl. May I hold out all that is valuable to me and allow You to use it. May people see You, not me. It's 9:02 in our world everyday. Give me forever eyes. Lord, "let's roll."

Decision Points

Brainstorm a list of ways you could contribute something that could be used to bring people information on who Jesus is. Offer your possessions for use to a church, a youth group, or a parachurch organization.

Make a list of people you know that don't know Christ yet. Next to each name, brainstorm a list of their interests and felt needs. Is there a tangible way you could begin taking Jesus' love to those on your list?

Now think of your community. Who are the people at highest risk in your town? Who are the "at risk" groups: single moms, minority children, the poor? Is there a way you could impact just *one* of those lives?

How can you take what is ordinary in your life and use it for the extraordinary purpose of proclaiming the love of God? Can your Christmas card include information on Jesus? Can your personal stationery have a verse at the bottom? Can you meet a new person at the gym, the ballpark, or the store instead of just hanging out with your same safe group of friends?

Pray and ask God to (1) show you people through His eyes and (2) give you a sense of urgency when dealing with people and their need to know Him personally.

Study Guide and Small Group Questions

$\mathcal{T}$his section is designed for the woman who wants to go to a deeper place with God. Each chapter will have a weeklong assignment followed by small group discussion questions. The assignment may be one question with many facets, or it may be several questions. As you work on digging out a few new truths each day on that topic, you'll discover God has led you through His Word, and you will have a fuller, deeper, and richer view of the chapter's topic. You can then choose to facilitate or participate in a small group that meets once a week and discusses the chapter, the Decision Points assignments, and the Deeper Place adventure with God. You may decide to do the activities and discuss them with a trusted friend, mentor, daughter, daughter-in law, or spouse. The questions will simply help facilitate a discussion.

Chapter 1: Decide to Decide

A Deeper Place

Read the book of Ruth. In chapter 1, note the deep pain Naomi must have felt. What was the cause of her pain? What is the pain in your life right now? Often, for women, our pain is connected to our self-concept or those vital relationships that feed our view of ourselves. Naomi was so depressed, angry, and hurt that she even changed her name to outwardly mark the bitterness she felt inwardly. Naomi made a very important choice in chapter 1. She went back, back to the place she knew God would meet her, back to a place where people would point her to God, back to a place she knew to be a source of provision for her physically, emotionally, and spiritually. When life becomes confusing, go back.

Where are those places you know you heard God speak into your life? If you are feeling used up, unappreciated, or negative about your life, think of a time when you felt the pleasure of God. Close your eyes. Think of a time when you felt you rested in Him. I think one of the reasons swimming is so therapeutic for me is that when things became rough at my house while I was growing up, I would head out to the back pasture with my Bible and sit, dangling my feet into the cool creek water as I read, prayed, and talked to God. It was my personal oasis. I sensed God's pleasure as I sat and enjoyed His presence. I would encourage you to find a place where you can go to spend time alone with God when you are stressed out. Make it a place where you can remove yourself from any surrounding distractions. Make it a place where you can come to Him alone to share what is on your mind and heart. He tells us to come to Him when we are weary and heavy-laden, and He'll give us rest (Matthew 11:28-29 NASB). The key idea is to surrender. Give up your yoke for the one He has designed for you. What are you carrying that feels too heavy? What negative thoughts about yourself are you hearing that you'd like to have Him replace? Do you long to hear His applause, feel His approval? In a quiet time read the following verses and then ask yourself, *Because God is already doing all these things for me, will He not meet my needs now?* (Luke 15:10; John 14:2-3; Matthew 11:28-30; Revelation 21–22). Write a letter to Jesus. Tell Him all the heavy, negative things in the yoke you've been carrying. Tell Him how you felt as you surrendered, as you read the verses. Tell Him what you'd like to see happen in your life as a result of this study.

Questions to Pull the Pieces Together

1. Think of the last compliment you received. What was it for? Was it an external compliment: "Nice dress!" or "Your hair looks great!" or was it an internal compliment of your character: "You are so thoughtful" or "You are such a faithful friend." Try to describe how you feel when you are given each kind of compliment.

2. Talk about your answer to the *Decision Points* assignment. How would you describe a woman "who has it all"? How is the description different from your life right now? Do you think it is possible to "have it all"? Why or why not? Describe a time when you compared yourself to someone else or your life to her life. When was it? How did you feel as a result of comparing? Over the next several days, read the following verses about handling envy and jealousy:

Proverbs 14:30	Proverbs 23:17	Proverbs 24:1-2
1 Corinthians 13:4	Titus 3:3-8	James 3:13–4:3
1 Peter 2:1-3	Romans 13:13-14	1 Corinthians 3:3-9
Romans 12:14-21	Galatians 5:19-25	
2 Corinthians 12:20–13:8		

   Come up with a new plan to use when you are tempted to compare. Explain how you will handle those negative feelings the next time they arise.

3. What is your definition of significance? This chapter makes the case that if you see yourself from God's perspective, you will have a more accurate view of what is significant, of what pleases Him. Why do you think knowing how God sees you will impact your thinking in the coming weeks?

4. Do you have a specific area that you feel disappointed in, or do you think specific people are disappointed in you right

now? Pray with someone and commit those areas to God for His care as you work your way through this book.

Chapter 2: Decide to Be Authentic

A Deeper Place

Let's look at a true/false comparison. We'll start with false.

False. Read the entire book of Ecclesiastes. Solomon, the wisest man in history, chose to not believe God for his source of significance. Underline and mark false sources of significance in the margin of your Bible with an "F" for false. List areas of false significance you see in Solomon's life. What are the negative results for each area? What was Solomon's overall state of mind as a result of embracing false sources of significance? Which source of false significance are you most tempted to rely on instead of God? Are there any words of wisdom from Solomon that can help you when you are tempted to embrace a false source of significance?

True. Create your own love letter from God. First list any known weaknesses, footholds, or sources for false significance you have embraced. Write down key words that describe these areas.

Now next to each, write a few key words that are the opposite of these negative words. Look up verses in the Bible using the positive words. Try to find verses that describe God with terms similar to the positive traits listed. Choose your favorite five to ten verses and string them together. If you'd like, personalize the verses so the message seems to be coming straight from God to you. (See the example in the Decision Points section.)

Questions to Pull the Pieces Together

1. What are the common sources for significance you see promoted on television and in magazines? Do the media make you feel significant or insignificant? How? Why?

2. Think back on how you were raised. Were there any children's stories, either positive or negative, that helped form your

identity? Any things your family told you that formed a misconception of significance in your thinking?

3. What area of false significance are you most vulnerable to believing and embracing?

4. Considering all the examples in the chapter and the example of Solomon, what is the outcome if one continues to embrace false sources of significance?

Chapter 3: Decide to Get Over It

A Deeper Place

Read the story of King Saul's life (1 Samuel 9–16; 18–19; 23:7-28; 31:1-6). Try to diagram his downward progression. What key decisions did he make that propelled him in such a destructive pattern?

How about you? Can you identify your dark side and what will happen if you don't address it, keep it in check, or grow in victory over it?

Questions to Pull the Pieces Together

1. Name some modern-day leaders, stars, or celebrities who have not dealt with their baggage, their dark side. What is the result you are seeing in their lives?

2. "Our past influences our future." How do you think your upbringing or your own past choices have affected how you see yourself today?

3. What encouragement did you gain from learning that God already sees your imperfections and still loves you? How does this motivate you to want to open up your heart and allow God to grow you up in those imperfect areas?

4. Which Decision Points assignment did you complete? How do you feel now that you have taken a step forward to address this area?

Chapter 4: Decide to Turn Up the Truth

A Deeper Place

Embracing His choosing. Read these verses on being chosen. Did you find any new insights or applications you can make that will help you in your life this week?

John 13:18	Colossians 3:12	Acts 22:14
1 Thessalonians 1:4	Romans 8:33	James 2:5
Romans 11:5	1 Peter 1:2	Ephesians 1:11
1 Peter 2:9	Colossians 1:27	

Failure from God's perspective. Read the following verses on failure. What causes failure in God's eyes and how does He handle it? How does this help you handle failure?

Matthew 26:41	Hebrews 4:11	Luke 8:13
2 Peter 1:10	Romans 3:23	2 Peter 3:17
1 Corinthians 10:12	1 Timothy 6:9	

Questions to Pull the Pieces Together

1. What kind of envelope do you think you are?

2. What do you think keeps you from being God's envelope?

3. Do you have a method for sharing His hope that you are comfortable with? (As in *The Four Spiritual Laws, The Bridge, The Roman Road, The Wordless Book* or a bracelet of different colors that reminds you of the parts of the gospel message.) Visit a Christian bookstore and find a tool you are comfortable using to share about your relationship with God. (Bring it to the small group.)

4. Did you learn anything that will help you handle criticism?

5. What did you learn that will help you handle the fear of failure or recovering from failure?

6. Think of someone who could use the message of hope. Put something in an envelope and mail some encouragement from God to someone this week.

   (Note: If you are facilitating a group, this is a good week to remind people not to use real names or full names when describing circumstances that might put a person in a less than positive light.)

Chapter 5: Decide to Maximize Me

A Deeper Place

Below are some verses about time. What new insight or reminder of truth can you glean from each?

Genesis 1:3-5   1 Corinthians 4:5   Psalm 75:2
Galatians 6:9   Psalm 145:15   1 Peter 5:6
Ephesians 5:15-16   Ecclesiastes 8:5-6
Ecclesiastes 3:1-8,11,17

Look up the following verses that contain the words "vapor" or "mist." From the use of the words, what can you learn about the brevity of life from these verses?

Proverbs 21:6   Isaiah 44:22   Hosea 6:4; 13:3.

Look at Ecclesiastes 3:1-8, which says there is a time for everything. See if you can translate its meaning into a modern day example. For example: "A time to reap" might mean a time to collect the paycheck or bonus. Mark the "times" you have already experienced.

Questions to Pull the Pieces Together

1. According to the Expansionary Institute, the life expectancy of a woman is now 80 years. How many years does this leave you if that were to be true of you? How does this make you feel?

2. How does knowing you are "mist" free you and your thinking? How does it change your to-do list?

3. What legacy do you want to leave? What do you want said about you at your funeral?

4. If you'd like, read your personal mission statement out loud. How do you think this will help you make choices in the future?

5. When I was young, I was given the advice of "Do what you love to do, what you would do even if no one paid you to do, and you will always be successful." Do you agree or disagree?

6. How can maximizing your gift be a safeguard in case of death or divorce of a spouse? How does the view of wanting to have God use you to bring Him maximum glory impact your career decisions and choices?

Chapter 6: Decide to Be Successful in Each Season
A Deeper Place

Read these verses about our inheritance in Christ, our place in His family, and our place in the promise. How does knowing all this affect your view of yourself and of life?

Galatians 3:18	Colossians 3:23-24	Galatians 4:7
Hebrews 9:15	Hebrews 12:14-17	Ephesians 5:5
1 Peter 1:3-7	Colossians 1:12	
Ephesians 1:13-14,18-23		

God cares for you in every season of life. Read Psalm 139. What else does God know? Hebrews 13:8 says, "Jesus Christ is the same yesterday and today and forever." How is this a comfort or source of strength?

Questions to Pull the Pieces Together

1. Review the Five Seasons of Womanhood chart. Which season looks the most challenging and why?

2. Survey the group. Ask what advice were you given or what advice can you share that would help a woman safely travel through each season, using the season to grow rather than be overwhelmed by it.

3. Children and marriages also have stages and seasons. For women with children, what stage of child rearing was the most challenging? When do you think a marriage needs the most attention and why?

4. Single women also have life stage transitions. How can you bridge the emotional gap between singles and married couples to have friendships and support one another?

5. God's Word is like the safety harness when traversing the seasons of life. Have each group member share verses that have helped them in tough times. (It is also nice to have them bring the verse(s) and pass out copies so each member leaves with a card deck of verses that will help when life becomes challenging.)

Chapter 7: Decide to Live by Love

A Deeper Place

Look again at the verses in the "God's Will Made Clearer" section of this chapter. If your Bible lists cross-references for each verse in this section, look them up and write a one- or two-word synopsis that will help you remember what God wants from your life. By reading cross-references, you can gain a broader perspective on a subject. For example: Romans 12:1-2 talks about sanctification. Reading cross-references can shed an overall light of what a sanctified life might look like, especially when you follow the chain from verse to verse to verse, like clues to a treasure. Try to create a set of two to three questions for each verse in the "God's Will Made Clearer" list. It can become like a thermometer, checking your spiritual temperature and attitude toward God. For example: Because I am sanctified, I ask myself, "Am I guarding what I see, hear, and participate in so that the flame of light in me is fanned instead of extinguished?"

Questions to Pull the Pieces Together

1. Which tool of Satan's guilt works best on you?

2. How can knowing you are salt and light help to combat that tool?

3. When do you have the hardest time maintaining your personal healthy boundaries?

4. List the top ten people who have earned more right to your time. What is one boundary you can set that will ensure they have greater access to you? For example: A personal assistant can put calls from your kids through to you, no questions asked. You can get a cell phone that *only* your kids or your spouse can use to reach you.

5. What did you learn about God's voice that can help you discern between bad guilt and good conviction?

Chapter 8: Decide to Take Good Care of Me

A Deeper Place

Read the verses below about the temple Solomon built for God. For each reference listed, write a two- to-five-sentence synopsis that reminds you of what the temple is or how it is to be treated.

1 Kings 5:3-6	1 Kings 5:13-18	1 Kings 6:1-38
1 Kings 7:13-51	1 Kings 8:1-66	

What was God's response?

1 Kings 9:1-9

Second Chronicles 2–7 cross-references this same event. Are there any new or different insights from this passage?

How do these verses impact the way you see yourself, knowing that you are referred to as the temple of the Holy Spirit?

Read these verses on the Sabbath. Make a brief note of what information is in the verse. Are there any lifestyle changes you want to make as a result?

Exodus 16:23,25-26	Exodus 31:14-16	Leviticus 16:31
Leviticus 23:3,32	Leviticus 25:4	Isaiah 58:13-14
Matthew 12:1-12	John 5:1-17	

David was a man whose life was stressful. How do the psalms describe rest?

Psalm 16:9	Psalm 55:6	Psalm 62
Psalm 91	Psalm 116	

What did Jesus say about rest?

Matthew 11:28-29   Mark 6:31

What do the New Testament authors have to say about the way to handle heavy burdens, anxieties, and stress?

Acts 15:25-29	1 Peter 5:7	1 Thessalonians 2:9
Hebrews 13:17	Philippians 4:6-7	2 Thessalonians 3:8
2 Corinthians 11:9; 12:13-14		

Are there any commonalities between what David, Jesus, and the other authors said?

Questions to Pull the Pieces Together
1. What causes you stress?

2. Knowing you are the temple of God, are there any bad habits you need to quit or good habits you need to start?

3. Which gift do you need to most give yourself permission to receive? (Emotional connection, contentment, physical care, prayer, celebration, or hope?)

4. Share some things off your personal celebration list. Choose one to do today. If you did any last week, how did it make you feel? Why?

5. Did you learn anything from the Deeper Place that will impact your lifestyle?

6. Choose an accountability partner who will ask you every-time she sees you in the next month, "Are you taking care of the temple?"

Chapter 9: Decide to Be Daring

A Deeper Place

In the section below, mark every reference to who Jesus is with a cross. Mark every reference to who Jesus says you are with a heart. Underline all references to "remain," "stay," and "abide." Circle any promises or results of remaining, abiding, etc. What new insight or reminder did this activity bring to your mind?

John 15:1-16

"I am the true vine, and my Father is the gardener. [2] He cuts off every branch in me that bears no fruit, while every branch that does bear fruit he prunes so that it will be even more fruitful. [3] You are already clean because of the word I have spoken to you. [4] Remain in me, and I will remain in you. No branch can bear fruit by itself; it must remain in the vine. Neither can you bear fruit unless you remain in me.

[5] "I am the vine; you are the branches. If a man remains in me and I in him, he will bear much fruit; apart from me you can do nothing. [6] If anyone does not remain in me, he is like a branch that is thrown away and withers; such branches are picked up, thrown into the fire and burned. [7] If you remain in me and my words remain in you, ask whatever you wish, and it will be given you. [8] This is to my Father's glory, that you bear much fruit, showing yourselves to be my disciples.

[9] "As the Father has loved me, so have I loved you. Now remain in my love. [10] If you obey my commands, you will remain in my love, just as I have obeyed my Father's commands and remain in his love. [11] I have told you this so that my joy may be in you and that your joy may be complete. [12] My command is this: Love each other as I have loved you. [13] Greater love has no one than this, that he lay down his life for his friends. [14] You are my friends if you do what I command. [15] I no longer call you servants, because a servant does not know his master's business. Instead, I have called you friends, for everything that I learned from my Father I have made known to you. [16] You did not choose me, but I chose you and appointed you to go and bear fruit—fruit that will last. Then the Father will give you whatever you ask in my name.

Questions to Pull the Pieces Together

1. Can you think of a time when the fragrance of obedience impacted your life? Share it with the group.

2. What did you learn about the priority of the Word of God and its link to obedience?

3. Which Bible study method do you want to try so that God's word will be layered into your life?

4. Can you think of a time when either your sinful actions or someone else's resulted in "stinkin' thinkin'"? Can you give

an example of an outrageous saying or discussion that resulted because the person (you or another) wasn't walking in obedience? Share this with one other member and pray for each other.

5. When is it most difficult for you to obey?

6. Share your feelings about this phrase, "accountability only works if someone has a desire to obey." Agree or disagree and why?

Chapter 10: Decide to Leave a Legacy

A Deeper Place

Acts 1:8 says: "You will receive power when the Holy Spirit comes on you; and you will be my witnesses in Jerusalem, and in all Judea and Samaria, and to the ends of the earth."

We are witnesses of who Jesus is. Read about John the Baptist in John 1:1-37. What can you learn from John that can apply to your life today?

The epistles contain many references to light. Read the verses below and write who or what is the light and its purpose.

Romans 13:12	2 Corinthians 4:4	2 Corinthians 6:14
Ephesians 5:8-14	Hebrews 10:32	1 Peter 2:9
1 John 1:7; 2:9-10	1 Thessalonians 5:5	

Questions to Pull the Pieces Together

1. Describe the people who might see you as an ambassador. Brainstorm ways to be a more effective ambassador to them. (Learn their language, visit their homes, learn their needs, and so on.)

2. Choose one person and one way to be an ambassador. Begin praying for and scheduling time for that one individual.

Study Guide and Small Group Questions

3. How can you gain "forever eyes" for your world? What will help remind you of the priority of people?

4. Deciding to be a woman God can use is really about being usable. What attitudes or actions have you changed since beginning this study?

5. How has your self-concept changed? Which "You Are" was most meaningful to you and why?

6. How do you think seeing yourself more accurately, from God's point of view, helps you make better decisions?

7. List the ten best decisions you think God wants you to make in order to be all He wants you to become.

$\mathcal{N}$otes

Chapter 1—Deciding to Decide

1. Pam Farrel, *Hats Off to You* (Eugene, OR: Harvest House Publishers, 1999), p. 28.
2. Women of Faith conference, San Diego, CA, July 1998.
3. Lorraine Glennon, ed., *100 Most Important Women of the 20th Century* (Des Moines: Ladies Home Journal Books, 1998), p. 113.
4. John Robinson and Geoffrey Godbey, *A Time for Life* (University Park, PA: Pennsylvania State Press, 1997), p. 44.
5. Os Guinness, *The Call* (Nashville, TN: Word, 1998), p. 46.

Chapter 2—Decide to Be Authentic

1. Dana Demetre, *The Lifestyle Solution Workbook* (San Diego, CA: LifeStyle Dimensions, 1998), p. 43.
2. Ibid., p. 43.
3. See 1 Chronicles 29:10-13; Psalm 28:7; Psalm 121:3; 2 Timothy 1:12; 1 Thessalonians 5:24; 2 Corinthians 1:20.

Chapter 3—Decide to Get Over It

1. Gary McIntosh and Samuel Rima, Sr., *Overcoming the Dark Side of Leadership: The Paradox of Personal Dysfunction* (Grand Rapids, MI: Baker Books, 1979), pp. 11-12.
2. Ibid., p. 14.

Chapter 4—Decide to Turn Up the Truth

1. Poor Man's College Quotation search at www.starlingtech.com/quotes.
2. www.yahoo.com/reference/quotations.
3. Ruth Tucker and Walter Liefeld, *Daughters of the Church* (Grand Rapids, MI: Academie Books, 1987), p. 336.
4. Ibid., p. 337.
5. Ibid., p. 338.

6. J.I. Packer, *Knowing God* (Downers Grove, IL: InterVarsity Press, 1973), p. 37.

7. In "God's Statement of Love to Us," all Scriptures used are from the International Children's Bible, New Century Version, unless otherwise noted.

Chapter 5—Decide to Maximize Me

1. "Dilbert," United Feature Syndicate, Inc., 1997 Day Runner, Inc.

2. Pam Farrel, *Woman of Influence* (Downers Grove, IL: InterVarsity Press, 1996), p. 103.

3. Os Guinness, *The Call* (Nashville, TN: Word, 1998), p. 79.

4. Ibid., p. 45.

5. Dr. Archibald Hart, *Adrenaline and Stress* (Dallas, TX: Word, 1995), p. 138.

6. Ibid., p. 177.

Chapter 6—Decide to Be Successful in Each Season

1. Patsy Clairmont, Barbara Johnson, Marilyn Meberg, and Luci Swindoll, *Joy Breaks* (Grand Rapids, MI: Zondervan Publishing, 1997), p. 241.

2. John Robinson and Geoffrey Godbey, *A Time for Life* (University Park, PA: Pennsylvania State Press, 1997), p. 110.

3. www.lifetimetv.com.

4. Kim Clark and Lenore Schiff, "Do You Really Work More?" April 29, 1996, www.pathfinder.com/fortune.html.

5. www.prnewswire.com.

6. Robinson and Godbey, *A Time for Life*, p. xvii.

7. Ibid.

8. See http://slashdot.org/features/00/02/13/2257216.shtml.

9. Robinson and Godbey, *A Time for Life*, p. 34.

10. To locate this necklace, order at www.josh.org.

11. Brenda Hunter, *Where Have All the Mothers Gone?* (Grand Rapids, MI: Zondervan, 1982), pp. 92-93.

12. Ibid., p. 90.

Chapter 7—Decide to Live by Love

1. Naomi Beard, *Following Christ Beyond Your Cultural Walls*, Women's Ministry Symposium, March 1998, p. 49.

2. www.libertynet.org/~edcivic/welfheri.html.

3. Beard, *Following Christ*, p. 50.

4. www.libertynet.org/~edcivic/welfheri.html.

5. Beard, *Following Christ*, p. 51.

6. www.niaid.nih.gov/factsheets/womenhiv.htm.

7. Beard, *Following Christ*, p. 54.

8. www.ojp.usdoj.gov/ovc/ncvrw/2001/stat_over_12.htm.

9. www.pdxcityclub.org/report/domvio.htm#link2.

10. Lorraine Glennon, ed., *100 Most Important Women of the 20th Century* (Des Moines, IA: Ladies Home Journal Books, 1998), p. 20.

11. www.nationalcampaign.org/pr09.asp.

12. Miriam Neff and Debra Kingsporn, *Shattering Our Assumptions* (Minneapolis, MN: Bethany House, 1996), pp. 29-30.

13. Lauri McIntyre, NEWIM conference, Riverside, CA, February 5, 1999.

Chapter 8—Decide to Take Good Care of Me

1. Tom Peterson, *Living the Life You Were Meant to Live* (Nashville, TN: Thomas Nelson, 1998), p. 201.

2. Pastor to Pastor, *Budgets and Burnout*, audiotape vol. 1, 1993. Focus on the Family, Colorado Springs, CO 80995.

3. Dr. Archibald Hart, *Adrenaline and Stress* (Dallas, TX: Word Publishing, 1995), p.12.

4. Personal interview, February 1, 1999.

5. Dean Ornish, M.D., *Love and Survival* (New York, NY: HarperCollins Publishers, 1998), p. 25.

6. Ibid., p. 29.

7. J.S. House, K.R. Landis, and D. Umberson, "Social Relationships and Health," *Science*, 1998, p. 241:540-45.

8. L.G. Russek and G.E. Schwartz, "Perceptions of Parental Caring Predict Health Status in Midlife: A 35-Year Follow Up of the Harvard Mastery of Stress Study," *Psychosomatic Medicine*, 1997, 59 (2):144-49.

9. T.E. Oxman, D.H. Freeman, Jr., and E.D. Manheimer, "Lack of Social Participation or Religious Strength and Comfort as Risk Factors for Death after Cardiac Surgery in the Elderly," *Psychosomatic Medicine*, 1995, 57:5-15.

10. Ornish, *Love and Survival*, p. 53; For information on this research see, D. Spiegel, *Living Beyond Limits: New Hope and Help for Facing Life Threatening Illness* (New York, NY: Times Books, 1993).

11. J.W. Pennebaker, *Opening Up: The Healing Power of Confiding in Others* (New York, NY: William Morrow, 1990), pp. 118-19.

12. Ornish, *Love and Survival*, p. 95.

13. Hart, *Adrenaline and Stress*, pp. 96-97.

14. Ornish, *Love and Survival*, pp. 59-60.

15. Interview with Michael Roizen, M.D., January 12, 1999. The RealAge Company has a website at www.realage.com.

16. Dana Demetre, *The Lifestyle Solution Workbook* (San Diego, CA: LifeStyle Dimensions, 1998), p. 41.

17. Ibid., p. 86.

18. Ibid., p. 147.

19. Virtue, *Make Your Home a House of Prayer,* January 1999.

20. USA Today WWW search *Health Magazine.*

21. Send them my way at mliving@webcc.net.

22. Karen Peterson, *A Chuckle a Day Does Indeed Help Keep Ills at Bay,* www.usato-day.com.

23. Ibid.

24. Hart, *Adrenaline and Stress,* p. 28.

Chapter 9—Decide to Be Daring

1. *Strong's Exhaustive Concordance WordSearch.*

2. Walk Thru the Bible ministries: www.walkthru.org.

3. NEWIM conference, February 6, 1999.

4. Ibid.

5. Chosen Women conference, May 1997, Pasadena, CA.

Chapter 10—Decide to Leave a Legacy

1. What Would Jesus Do?

2. For underlying source material, see *The Teacher's Commentary,* 1983, Scripture Press Publications, Inc., licensed by Victor Books.

3. Ibid.

4. Ruth Tucker, *Stories of Faith* (Grand Rapids, MI: Daybreak Books, 1989), p. 312 and Ethel Waters web page "Colored Reflections."

5. Os Guinness, *The Call* (Nashville, TN: Word, 1998), p. 31.

6. Ibid., p. 20.

7. Mark 8:34

8. Romans 8:28

9. Galatians 5:13

10. Ephesians 4:4

11. Colossians 3:15

12. 1 Thessalonians 4:7

13. Hebrews 9:15

14. 1 Peter 2:21

15. 1 Peter 3:9

16. Mark 9:35

17. Robertson's Word Pictures, WordSearch

18. Tucker, *Stories of Faith,* p. 94.

19. Ibid., p. 96.

20. Ibid., p. 127.

To contact Pam Farrel, write to her at

Farrel Communications
3755 Avacado Blvd. #414
La Mesa, CA 91941

or e-mail her at

info@farrelcommunications.com

www.farrelcommunications.com

Other Harvest House Books
by Pam Farrell

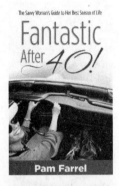

FANTASTIC AFTER FORTY!
Popular speaker and bestselling author Pam Farrel challenges and inspires the baby boomer generation of women with 40 unique ways to shape a fulfilling future, embrace God's truth, and uncover their unique purpose.

WOMAN OF CONFIDENCE
Nothing is more vital to a woman's self-confidence than her confidence in God. *Woman of Confidence* helps you understand that mustering up enough *self*-confidence is not the answer. Your ability to move through life with courage and boldness rests instead on your trust in the character, power, and strength of God.

**THE 10 BEST DECISIONS
A COUPLE CAN MAKE**
Bill and Pam Farrel, bestselling authors of Men Are Like Waffles—Women Are Like Spaghetti, lead you through the ten most influential decisions you can make in the areas of romance, communication, sex, family, and conflict resolution. Whether you are newlyweds or longtime marriage partners, you will learn to create a life together of trust, grace, and understanding. (Rerelease of *Every Marriage Is a Fixer Upper.*)

More Great Harvest House Books

THE POWER OF A PRAYING® WOMAN
by Stormie Omartian
Stormie's deep knowledge of Scripture and candid examples from her own prayer life will help you trust God with your deepest longings and cover every area of your life with prayer.

A WOMAN AFTER GOD'S OWN HEART®
by Elizabeth George
These Scripture-based principles will help you become God's woman of excellence, achieve a growing relationship with God, develop an active partnership with your husband, and make your home into a spiritual oasis.

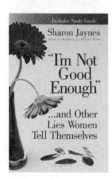

"I'M NOT GOOD ENOUGH"…AND OTHER LIES WOMEN TELL THEMSELVES
by Sharon Jaynes
Sharon Jaynes looks at the common lies women tell themselves and demonstrates how you can replace those lies with truth. Her book is a handy reference tool that will help you renew your mind and think God's thoughts rather than be swayed by the enemy's deceptions.

To learn more about books by Pam Farrel
and other Harvest House authors
or to read sample chapters, log on to our website:

www.harvesthousepublishers.com

HARVEST HOUSE PUBLISHERS

EUGENE, OREGON